No Naughties

This book is also available as a
large print edition (ISBN 978-0-9569867-2-6)

Find more recipes and information
on coping with restricted diets on

www.nonaughties.com

No Naughties

Sweet treats without sugar, wheat, gluten and yeast

Tarja Moles

Luscious Books

First published in Great Britain 2012 by Luscious Books

A CIP catalogue record for this book is available from the British Library

ISBN 978-0-9569867-1-9

Printed and bound in Great Britain by Lightning Source Ltd UK

The information provided in this book is not a substitute for professional medical care, advice or guidance by a doctor or other suitably qualified healthcare professional. It cannot be war-ranted that any information included in this book will meet your particular health or medical requirements. It is very important that you seek medical advice from a doctor or other suitably qualified healthcare professional if you have any concerns or questions about your health and diet.

Those who might be at risk from the effects of salmonella food poisoning (for example, elderly people, pregnant women, young children and those suffering from immune deficiency dis-eases) should consult their doctor with any concerns about eating raw eggs.

Where organisations and their websites are mentioned, these are provided for information only. The author or the publisher does not accept any responsibility for the content and/or advice they offer.

Many of the designations used by manufacturers and sellers to distinguish their products are claimed as trademarks. Where the publisher is aware of a trademark claim, such designa-tions, in this book, have initial capital letters.

In memory of Vic, my late father-in-law
who understood the importance of sweet treats

Contents

Foreword

One of the most enjoyable things about cooking is being able to create a wonderful culinary experience. It is important that people with special dietary requirements can have the same level of experience and enjoyment as everyone else.

I know first-hand how difficult it can be: my sister is affected by a dairy intolerance which triggers headaches or cold-like symptoms. But having a food allergy shouldn't hinder your relationship with food. It is all about finding what suits you and adapting dishes to your tastes.

At my Padstow restaurant, Number 6, I cook for customers with different allergies and dietary requirements every week, and accommodating all our customers' needs is something I feel very strongly about. Customers can pick what they want off the menu and the recipes are adjusted to suit each individual without compromising the care, attention and passion which go into all the other dishes.

Over the years I have taught myself the best ways to cater for people with dietary requirements. Food intolerances are a lot more common now, but fortunately there are so many ingredients out there which are great alternatives and which I would use – not just because of necessity – but because of the flavour. I would encourage anyone who has to cook for restricted diets, whether for themselves or other people, to experiment with the less well-known ingredients and enjoy the process of learning to cook differently.

With this book Tarja Moles has created some great recipes which enable people to enjoy the same treats as those without allergies. She has captured the importance of adapting dishes to suit individual circumstances and highlights how you can make your diet work for you, without losing the enjoyment of food and cooking.

Paul Ainsworth

A classically trained chef, Paul developed his skills in London under Gary Rhodes, Gordon Ramsay and Marcus Wareing. Moving to Padstow, Cornwall in 2006, Paul opened Number 6 with friends before taking sole occupancy in 2009. One of the most respected chefs in Cornwall, Paul won the dessert course on the BBC2 TV series Great British Menu in 2011.

www.paul-ainsworth.co.uk

Acknowledgements

I am grateful to Anna France for her meticulous editing and proof-reading. Thank you for all your hard work and being so generous with your time. Any mistakes in this book are, however, mine alone.

I would like to thank all those family members, friends and acquaintances who have been my guinea-pigs over the years. Your feedback has been invaluable. Especially, I would like to thank my mother-in-law Margaret who has faithfully sampled my sweet treats, even though it has at times meant eating different versions of the same pudding for weeks on end so that I could perfect a recipe.

Special thanks go to my husband David. Without your support and practical help it would not have been possible to write this book. I love you gazillions.

Food, like a loving touch or a glimpse of divine power, has that ability to comfort.

- Norman Kolpas

Introduction

Having a sweet tooth and being on a restrict-ed diet is a tricky combination. There have been countless times over the years when I have stood by patisserie windows and sali-vated over their cakes, or watched my friends eat the most amazing-looking puddings in restaurants without being able to have any myself. Ten years ago, when the number of my dietary intolerances increased, I was determined to find a way to satisfy my sweet tooth without the rest of my body suffering.

I began the process of developing cake and pudding recipes that are suitable for my gluten-free (and therefore also wheat-free), sugar-free, yeast-free, soya-free, peanut-free and low-lactose diet. I also did egg-free, dairy-free, nut-free, corn-free and vegan experiments to cater for some of my friends and family members.

The success of these experiments has been mixed, ranging from cakes that have even damaged the bin to puddings that have been served to numerous unsuspecting guests with-out them ever knowing there was no sugar in their desserts.

As the experiments have continued, I have figured out how the more unusual substitute ingredients work and, as a consequence, developed more and more scrumptious treats.

My aim has always been to make all treats taste as 'normal' as possible. Many ready-made gluten-free products have 'a gluten-free flavour'. If you've tried them, you'll know what I mean. I want to avoid this. Similarly, I don't want to use artificial sweeteners as these also tend to compromise the flavour, plus they may not be good for you anyway. Only treats that are truly delectable and natural are included in this book.

It can be difficult to stick to your diet if you have multiple dietary restrictions. You want to enjoy food and not be confined to eating boring things. This book aims to bring some spark and celebration into your life. Despite having to limit your diet it is possible to prepare and eat delicious food.

If you have only recently started following a special diet, you may feel like you've got to learn to cook and bake again from scratch. Don't be daunted by this prospect: doing things differently and learning about new foodstuffs can be a lot of fun. The recipes in this book are simple and easy to follow and the reward at the end is always a yummy treat!

Who is this book for?

An increasing number of people are following restricted diets. It's estimated that in the UK almost 1 in 20 people has diabetes, 1 in 100 suffers from coeliac disease, 1 in 50 has a food allergy which is potentially fatal, 1 in 4 experiences symptoms of irritable bowel syndrome (IBS) at some point in their lives and more than 1 in 10 are actually diagnosed with this condition.

Many have more than just one ingredient they need to avoid. For example, diabetics seem to be more susceptible to developing coeliac disease and those with allergies or intolerances often have several foodstuffs they can't eat. There are also others with various medical conditions – such as fibromyalgia, ME, chronic fatigue syndrome (CFS), candidiasis and autism spectrum disorders – who have found some relief to their symptoms by eliminating a number of specific foods from their diets.

A growing number of people have made a voluntary decision to restrict their diets.

As people become more health conscious, they're paying more attention to what they eat and this affects their food choices. Some limit their sugar intake to aid their oral health or to support their weight loss regimes. Others have found that they feel better if they avoid gluten, soya or other foodstuffs.

Regardless of your reasons for multiple dietary restrictions, this book can help you to enjoy sweet treats without those 'naughty' ingredients. Since my recipes stem from my many restrictions, anyone who can't eat gluten, wheat, refined sugar, yeast, soya and peanuts can find new ideas to satisfy their sweet tooth. Recipes without dairy, casein, lactose, eggs, nuts and corn are also included.

This book can also give you inspiration and ideas for preparing treats when family members have different dietary restrictions. If one can't eat wheat, another has diabetes and a third can't eat nuts, it's often simpler to prepare one dessert which everyone can enjoy as opposed to making three different ones. Similarly, you can find treats that are suitable for both adults' dinner parties and children's parties: instead of having to remember what is suitable for each of your guests, you can opt for making cakes and other sweet treats that are suitable for all.

This is my invariable advice to people: Learn how to cook - try new recipes, learn from your mistakes, be fearless, and above all have fun!
- Julia Child

How to use
this book

This book has a wide variety of recipes ranging from the super quick to the more elaborate desserts. However, even the treats that take a little longer to prepare are simple and easy to make. You don't need to be a patisserie chef to achieve delicious results!

The book is divided into sections based on suggestions of what kinds of treats could be eaten at different times of the day. You can, of course, make any treat at any time you wish.

You will find a recipe index at the back of the book which indicates the suitability of the recipes for different diets. However, this is only meant as a guide. You should always look at each recipe carefully in order to decide whether it's suitable for you. For example, if you're on an anti-candida diet, not all recipes are suitable at every stage of the diet. Diabetics should pay attention to the amount of fat and carbohydrates in the recipes and decide for themselves what the right portion should be.

To help you get to grips with making treats without many often-used ingredients, you can find general information on them at the beginning of the book. There is also information on where to shop for them as well as tips for successful treat making. Further suggestions for substitutions, what to do with leftovers, should there be any, and how to tweak the recipes to provide variety are given on the recipe pages.

At the end of the book you can find conversion tables if you prefer to use imperial measures instead of the metric ones given in recipes. There is also a list of resources on various medical conditions that might be helped by a special diet, relevant organisations and associations, online shops and 'free-from' products.

Treats bring sweetness to life. However, moderation is still something you might want to aspire to – difficult though it can be! Just as your taste buds will thank you for allowing yourself to enjoy cakes and puddings, your body will thank you for not over-doing it.

Enjoy your 'No Naughties' treats!

Disclaimer

Please note that I am not a medical doctor and this book is not meant as a substitute for professional medical care or advice. It merely contains information and recipe ideas that I have found useful in managing my own dietary restrictions. The information included in this book may not meet your particular health or medical requirements. If you have, or suspect that you may have, a medical condition that restricts your diet, seek advice from a doctor or other suitably qualified healthcare professional.

About ingredients

When I tell people about my dietary restrictions, often their initial reaction is to assume I can't eat anything. Although there are numerous ingredients and products that I have difficulty tolerating, this does not mean I can't treat myself. In fact, there are many ingredients nowadays that can be used as substitutes, and more 'free-from' products are coming to the market all the time.

This section looks at the 'naughty' ingredients as well as the substitutes that have been used in this book. Understanding how the different ingredients work is the first step towards being able to modify recipes successfully.

If you're interested in exploring any of the ingredients and products further, have a look at the Resources section to find out where to obtain more information.

Gluten and wheat

Gluten is a protein composite found in wheat, durum wheat, spelt, kamut, triticale, barley and rye. Oats may be contaminated by gluten due to the common practice of rotating wheat and oats crops in the fields. There is also the possibility of the two similar looking grains becoming mixed up during the manufacturing process. However, it is now possible to find gluten-free oats in supermarkets and health food shops.

Gluten has many useful purposes in baking. It makes the dough elastic and helps it to rise by holding in the gas bubbles formed by the leavening agent. When bread or cake is baked, gluten, with the help of starch, helps to provide the necessary structure for it to maintain its shape. It also provides bread with its chewy texture.

Given gluten's fundamental role in baking, how can we make cakes and other treats without it? Fortunately, it's role is not as crucial in cakes and sweet treats as it is in baking yeast breads. This doesn't mean that baking with gluten-free flour is without its challenges.

Gluten-free cakes and pastries are more likely to crumble if no gluten substitutes are added, but this is not necessarily a bad thing. For example, gluten-free short crust pastry is naturally flaky which is wonderful. More problematic is the fact that certain gluten-free baked goods won't brown as well in the oven as those made with ordinary wheat flour. There are ways around this, though, but it's good to get used to the idea that baked treats may look a little bit on the pale side.

The most frustrating issue with many gluten-free flours is that they don't generally taste as flavoursome as wheat flour. However, it is possible to bake tasty desserts by using other ingredients that add to the flavour and/or by using the right mixture of different flours.

There are a number of gluten-free flours and other substitutes that can be used instead of wheat flour. The recipes in this book include the following:

'Gluten Free Plain White Flour' and 'Gluten Free White Bread Flour' by Doves Farm

I like using ready-made gluten-free flour mixes as they take away the hassle of having to buy lots of different kinds of flour and then doing the mixing yourself. There are several brands of gluten-free flour mixes in the market nowadays, but the ones by Doves Farm are used in this book because they are so widely available in the UK. You can buy them in most supermarkets and health food shops, and you can also order them online, for example, on the Doves Farm website.

The plain white flour blend is made from rice, potato, tapioca, maize and buckwheat flours, so it's not suitable for people who can't eat corn. However, the bread flour variety does not contain any corn, but is a blend of rice, potato and tapioca flours with some added xantham gum.

Polenta

Polenta, also known as cornmeal or maize meal, is a yellow flour ground from corn. It has three consistencies depending on how it has been ground: coarse, medium and fine. All recipes in this book use fine polenta.

Large supermarkets tend to stock it either in their Italian grocery section or in the 'whole foods' or 'free-from' aisles. You may also find it in some ethnic shops, such as those specialising in Indian or Italian food.

No one is born a great cook, one learns by doing.

- Julia Child

Corn flour

Corn flour is the white and fine starch of the corn. It's often used in the recipes to thicken liquid. You can find it on the baking aisle in most supermarkets.

Ground almonds

Ground almonds are a very good wheat flour substitute as they taste much nicer than many gluten-free flours. They also make cakes deliciously succulent and soft. Supermarkets sell ground almonds on the baking aisle. If you prefer, you can also buy whole almonds, remove their skins and grind them yourself.

Raising agents

All of the recipes in this book are yeast-free. Instead, baking powder and bicarbonate of soda are used as raising agents. In some recipes even these are not used, but air is incorporated into batters, for example, by whisking eggs or egg whites.

Standard baking powder is not gluten-free, so read the labels carefully when you're shopping. Bicarbonate of soda, also known as sodium bicarbonate, sodium bicarb, bicarb soda or simply bicarb, is naturally gluten-free.

You can find gluten-free baking powder and bicarbonate of soda on the baking aisle or the 'free-from' aisle in most supermarkets as well as in health food shops.

Sugar and sweeteners

None of the recipes in this book uses ordinary sugar, or sucrose. Instead, the following natural sweeteners are used:

Xylitol

Xylitol, which is most often used in this book, is a natural sweetener. It's found in many fibrous fruits and vegetables, but its purified and manufactured form, which looks like a white crystalline substance resembling ordinary sugar, is usually made from birch sap.

Unlike many artificial sweeteners, xylitol doesn't have an unpleasant aftertaste. It has a similar sweetness level and bulk as sugar, but it tastes slightly different, bringing a pleasant cooling sensation into your mouth as it dissolves. It complements any mint- or citrus-flavoured treats as it heightens the feeling of freshness already present in these flavours. You won't always notice the coolness, though, especially if xylitol is just one of many ingredients in your treats.

Xylitol has been used for sweetening in Europe since the 19th century. The first large-scale manufacturing of xylitol began in Finland in 1974 when sugar-free chewing gums were introduced in the country. Soon afterwards the United States followed suit, and since then other countries have gradually adopted its use. You can now find xylitol in chewing gums and confectionary, dietetic and diabetic foods, toothpastes, mouthwashes, cosmetics and pharmaceutical products, such as various syrups and chewable tablets.

The reason for xylitol's increasing popularity can be found in the number of its health benefits:

– It only has 40% of the calories of ordinary sugar, so it can aid weight loss.

– It has a low glycaemic index and it is metabolised independently of insulin. This means that when eating foods sweetened with xylitol the sharp increase in blood sugar levels and the associated insulin response to sucrose consumption are significantly reduced. Therefore, xylitol is usually suitable for diabetics and those following low glycaemic index or low glycaemic load diets.

– It does not cause tooth decay like sugar does, so it's better for oral health.

– With regard to candida overgrowth, xylitol does not feed candida and other yeasts like most other forms of sugar do, but actually inhibits them. However, this is only the case with xylitol that has been made from birch.

Xylitol behaves in many ways similarly to ordinary sugar in cooking and baking, although there are certain differences:

– It does not caramelise and therefore it won't make a nice caramel sauce or syrup.

– It can't be used to bake anything that uses yeast as the raising agent, such as bread, because yeast can't metabolise it. Since all the recipes in this book are yeast-free, this is not an issue.

– Baking times are a little bit longer than with treats sweetened with ordinary sugar.

Besides these, you would hardly notice the difference when preparing your sweet treats.

The potential downside of xylitol for human beings is its laxative effect if used in excess. Generally it is advised that adults tolerate 40 g of xylitol daily, but the amount can vary depending on individual susceptibility and weight. So, if a recipe uses a lot of xylitol, do not be tempted to scoff the treat all on your own at once!

Xylitol is only intended for human consumption. It's toxic to dogs and ferrets, and possibly also to cows, goats, rabbits and other animals. So **do not feed your pets any treats containing xylitol,** and make sure your children don't do this either. If your dog happens to eat something with xylitol in it, contact the vet immediately.

There are several brands of xylitol to choose from, such as, Total Sweet (previously known as Perfect Sweet), XyloBrit, Xylo-Sweet and Xylitol UK. You can buy them online, in health food shops or large supermarkets where the bags are usually found either on the 'free-from' aisle or next to sugar and other sweeteners.

If you're avoiding sugar because of candida, make sure you use xylitol that is made from birch and not corn. Total Sweet, Xylitol UK and XyloBrit are always made from birch.

Sweet Freedom

Sweet Freedom is a sweetening syrup made from three natural ingredients: apples, grapes and carob. It has 25% fewer calories than ordinary sugar and a low glycaemic load. It can be used as a honey substitute and, in fact, it is currently the bestselling vegan honey alternative in the UK.

There are two kinds of Sweet Freedom, both of which come in a squeezable bottle. The milder tasting one is called Sweet Freedom Original and the richer one is Sweet Freedom Dark. In this book Sweet Freedom Original is used. If you prefer a more syrupy flavour, feel free to use Sweet Freedom Dark instead.

You can buy Sweet Freedom products online, in health food shops and in large supermarkets. They are located either on the 'free-from' aisle or next to sugar and other sweeteners.

No-added-sugar fruit spreads

Some recipes use no-added-sugar fruit spreads to add sweetness. Well-known brands include St. Dalfour and Meridian, the former usually tasting sweeter than the latter. The St. Dalfour spreads are sold in most supermarkets and they sit on shelves together with other jams. The bigger supermarkets tend to stock a wider variety of flavours. Both brands can be found in most health food shops.

There are some diabetic fruit spreads which are sweetened either with fructose or artificial sweeteners. These usually taste a lot sweeter than the naturally sweetened fruit spreads. Although I have not used these in the recipes, you can of course decide for yourself which ones to use.

No additional sugar needed

This book includes some recipes where no additional sugar is needed at all, or adding any one of the above sugar substitutes is optional. Whenever fruit or dried fruit are used in recipes, they bring their own natural sweetness to the treats. Generally, the treats in the book are not intensely sweet to avoid masking the natural flavours of other ingredients.

Dairy

Milk and substitutes

If you can't use milk for whatever reason, there is a range of alternative products. If you're lactose intolerant, but are happy to continue using dairy products that have been processed to make their digestion easier, you can use lactose-free milk, such as Arla's Lactofree milk. You may also be able to tolerate goat's milk.

Completely dairy-free milk alternatives include rice drinks, such as Rice Dream, and soya drinks. There are also oat drinks, but these may not be gluten-free. None of the recipes in this book use soya or oat milk, but you're welcome to use them if they suit your diet.

The non-dairy milk substitutes do not taste the same as milk although the dairy alternatives are more like it. When making treats, this can mean that the outcome may not taste the same as when milk is used. Of course, you may like a particular milk alternative and prefer its taste to that of milk, in which case the taste difference is not a problem. However, if you're not used to the milk alternatives, the flavour may initially be unfamiliar.

You can find lactose-free and goat's milk as well as soya, rice and oat drinks in most supermarkets, although there is more choice in larger supermarkets. The UHT varieties are found together with other UHT milk, and the fresh ones are with the refrigerated milk. Health food shops also stock a range of milk alternatives as do online stores.

Cream

Cream has a lower lactose level than milk, which is why some lactose intolerant people find they are able to have some cream without problems. Arla manufactures Lactofree cream which can be used for whipping, pouring and cooking. You can buy it in health food shops and on the dairy aisle in large supermarkets.

There are some non-dairy cream alternatives for sale, but, in my opinion, their taste is not as nice as the taste of real cream. These substitutes may also contain sugar, fructose, casein and/or oats contaminated with gluten which rule out their use in certain diets. If none of these ingredients are a problem for you, or you find one that doesn't have any 'naughty' ingredients, feel free to experiment. Be mindful, though, that the recipe may not always work as well with a non-dairy cream substitute.

Natural yogurt

Natural probiotic yogurt, or yogurt with bio-cultures, is often tolerated by people with lactose intolerance. Plain goat's yogurt with bio-cultures may also be suitable. Non-dairy alternatives for natural yogurt include plain soya yogurt. However, it may contain added sugar.

I have used full fat natural yogurt with bio-cultures or Greek yogurt with bio-cultures in the recipes as I don't like the low fat ones, but feel free to use low fat varieties if you prefer. You can find yogurts online, in health food shops and on the dairy aisle in supermarkets. Most of these places also stock goat's yogurt.

Butter

Butter gives a lovely flavour to puddings and cakes. All the recipes in this book use real (not spreadable) unsalted butter.

If you can't eat any dairy products, non-dairy vegetable margarine can be used instead. You can find it in most supermarkets and health food shops. However, when choosing a packet, make sure it's suitable for baking as some margarines are only meant to be used as spreads.

Cream cheese

Some of the recipes use cream cheese. If you need to avoid lactose, use Arla's Lactofree Soft White Cheese. You can find it in health food shops and on the dairy aisle in large supermarkets.

Quark

Quark is a popular ingredient in both sweet and savoury foods in many European countries. It's a little bit like cream cheese, but its fat content is low and protein content is high. About 80% of its protein is casein. If you don't tolerate dairy, lactose or casein but you're fine with soya, you could try using smooth tofu instead. Since tofu's flavour is stronger than that of quark, you may need to increase the amount of sweetener in the treat.

Eggs

I have used large eggs in all of the recipes and have not tried any egg substitutes as some contain soya and they don't work in all recipes. If you're allergic to eggs and want to try egg substitutes, the rule of thumb is that the fewer eggs there are in the recipe, the better the chance that the egg substitute will work. You can find egg substitutes online and in health food shops.

Elderly people, pregnant women, young children and those suffering from immune deficiency may want to avoid eating raw eggs. They should consult their GP with any concerns they have with regard to the matter.

Egg whites

When you're making custard or custard-based desserts, you will have egg whites left over. If you are not planning to use them immediately, you can freeze them for later use. Follow your freezer manufacturer's instructions.

Nuts

None of the recipes in this book contain peanuts, but a variety of other nuts are used. As mentioned previously, ground almonds, as well as other nuts, function well as a flour substitute, so this is mostly how they have been used. When nuts have been used as decoration, you can leave these out if you wish.

You can buy nuts online, in supermarkets and health food shops. Asian and other ethnic supermarkets also sell all sorts of nuts, often at a cheaper price. Always check the label and make sure you buy plain nuts, not with any flavourings or added salt.

Chocolate and cocoa

There are different kinds of sugar-free chocolates available in shops and online. Some use artificial sweeteners, maltitol, lactitol and/or sorbitol. Others, like Special Recipe and Holex, use fructose. The one that is used in this book is chocolate sweetened by xylitol. There are two brands currently available: Plamil's No Added Sugar Chocolate and Xylitol UK's chocolate. Both use xylitol extracted from birch. Although there is a variety of flavours, for instance, mint, orange and coffee, it's the plain chocolate that is used in the recipes throughout.

If you find Plamil's No Added Sugar Chocolate too dark, you could use Plamil's No Added Sugar Alternative to Milk Chocolate instead. However, this won't be suitable if you can't have soya. You can also try the milky varieties of the artificially sweetened or fructose-sweetened chocolates, but bear in mind that the fructose-sweetened chocolate may turn hard when baked.

If, in contrast, you like your chocolate treats extra dark, you could use 100% chocolate. This is, as the name indicates, genuinely plain dark chocolate without anything added to it. In the UK those produced by Hotel Chocolat and Willie's Cacao are the easiest to get hold of. If you decide to use it, remember that its taste is extremely bitter and therefore you may not need as much of it as the recipe states. You may also want to add some extra sweetener (like xylitol) to compensate for the bitterness.

You can buy xylitol (and other sugar-free) chocolate in health food shops and online. Some supermarkets also stock it. The cheapest way is to order Plamil's No Added Sugar Chocolate Catering Drops on their website. This is a 1 kg bag of small chocolate drops. They are really handy when baking as they're ready to use and you won't have to do any chopping first.

If you don't want to use chocolate, you can try carob instead. You may have to experiment a little and adjust the amount of sweetener in the recipe. You can find carob in health food shops and online.

Cocoa powder

Whenever cocoa powder is included as an ingredient in a recipe, you should use 100% natural cocoa. Don't use the powders meant for hot chocolate drinks: these are not strong enough, plus they will have sugar and other ingredients added to them.

You can find cocoa powder online, in health food shops and supermarkets, either on the baking aisle or next to the hot chocolate drinks.

Vanilla

All the recipes in this book that need the flavour of vanilla use natural vanilla extract as opposed to vanilla essence. The distillation process removes any gluten that may be in the extract, so it is safe for gluten-free diets. Feel free to use vanilla pods if you wish. The reason they have not been used in the recipes is that they are more expensive and require more preparation than the extract.

You can find vanilla extract online, in health food shops and on supermarkets' baking aisles. Always read the label carefully: it's very easy to pick up a bottle of vanilla essence instead of the extract.

Agar flakes

Agar can be used as a vegan gelling agent. Although it's not quite as versatile as gelatine, it has one superior quality: it sets much faster.

You can buy agar flakes in health food shops and some large supermarkets where they're often stocked on the same shelf with Japanese foods.

Mayonnaise

One of the recipes (Chocolate brownies) requires mayonnaise. Many brands contain sugar, so check the labels carefully. You can find sugar-free ones in large supermarkets, usually on the 'free-from' aisle, but sometimes also next to the ordinary mayonnaise. Health food shops also stock sugar- and egg-free mayonnaise as do several online shops, such as Plamil.

Cut my pie into four pieces, I don't think I could eat eight.

- Yogi Berra

Shopping for ingredients

When buying ingredients, make sure you always read the labels. For example, some dried fruit - like cranberries - are sold both with and without added sugar. So if sugar is a problem for you, make sure you pick up the right packet.

Sometimes the products you've been using for a long time may change their ingredients. Even if you have used a product before, always double-check what's on the ingredients list. This is particularly important when you notice that the packaging has changed as this could indicate that the recipe has changed as well.

Supermarkets

There is an increasing number of 'free-from' products available in supermarkets. It seems that every time I do my weekly shopping there are new products and ingredients to try.

This is great news for people with dietary restrictions.

Some supermarkets are better than others in terms of offering the required ingredients for the recipes in this book. Waitrose is generally excellent as you can get almost everything under the same roof. Large Sainsbury's and Tesco's are also very good. So, if you tend to do your weekly shop in one of these supermarkets, it's likely you won't have to search for many ingredients anywhere else.

Health food shops

All the unusual ingredients in this book can be found in health food shops. In general, the larger the shop, the better the variety. However, if your local health food shop is small and doesn't stock the products you need, ask if they could order the required items for you. Usually they are more than happy to help.

Ethnic food shops

Ethnic food shops, especially Asian ones, sell some of the ingredients used in the recipes. They are particularly good for different kinds of nuts and fresh fruit.

Online shopping

You can find all the ingredients used in the recipes in this book online and have them delivered to your home. You can either use health food shopping websites or supermarket shopping websites (see the Resources section for more details). Although it's possible to grab some really good bargains online, remember that you may have to pay a delivery charge.

This recipe is certainly silly. It says to separate the eggs, but it doesn't say how far to separate them.

- Gracie Allen

Tips for making successful treats

Be prepared

Before you start, read through the recipe. Check that you have all the required ingredients and equipment. Many of the substitute ingredients can't be bought in your nearby corner shop at the last minute, so decide in advance which recipe you're going to make and get yourself organised.

Get ready

At the start of each treat-making session, get all the ingredients and equipment ready. Measure the dry ingredients, chop the dried fruit or nuts, melt the butter, squeeze the lemons and grate their zest – basically, do whatever needs doing so that once you start mixing the ingredients together, you can just add them as you go along as opposed to trying to measure and chop and melt and mix all at the same time.

Measurements

It's important to be precise when weighing and measuring the ingredients. A teaspoon or a tablespoon of something is always a level spoonful, unless otherwise stated.

The measurements in this book are given in grams and millilitres. If you prefer imperial or American measures, you can find conversion tables at the back of the book. However, beware that mixing metric and imperial measures in one recipe may lead to a disaster, so decide which one you want to use and stick to that.

Sifting flour

It's recommended that you always sift the flour through a sieve before mixing it with other ingredients. This will help to break up any lumps as well as incorporate air into the batter. You should also always sift cocoa powder as it tends to get lumpy in the container.

Mixing ingredients

It's important not to over- or under-mix when preparing treats. The recipes will tell you how much you should mix and in what way.

Whipping cream

If you want to whip cream, it must contain at least 35% fat. Single cream's fat content is lower and therefore it's not suitable for whipping. Choose either double cream or whipping cream. If you want to avoid lactose, Arla's Lactofree cream will work well, too.

You can whip cream either with an electric whisk or a hand whisk. I usually use an electric whisk for volumes over 300 ml and a hand whisk for smaller volumes. Make sure you do not overdo the whipping. Stop when soft peaks form and the cream is fluffy. If you whip too much, the cream acquires a more solid texture and will be more difficult to spread.

Whisking egg whites

I would advise using an electric whisk for whisking egg whites as it requires less time and effort. However, you will get a good result by using a hand whisk, provided you don't mind whisking for quite a while.

Always use a fresh whisk and bowl. This will help the egg whites to yield as large a volume as possible. Since plastic bowls may retain fat and grease, it's advisable to use a metal or glass bowl.

To test if the egg whites are stiff enough, turn the bowl upside down and see whether the egg whites stay in the bowl and do not move at all. Be careful not to overbeat them, though, as the air will start to escape, leading to loss of volume.

Folding

To fold means to gently stir ingredients together in a way that allows as few air bubbles as possible to escape from the mixture. It's best to use a metal spoon when doing this. It cuts cleanly into the batter and avoids most of the air from escaping.

When you incorporate whisked egg whites into a batter, it's good to start by just folding in one spoonful first. This helps to loosen the mixture and it becomes easier to fold in the rest.

Beating butter and xylitol together

This refers to mixing butter and xylitol until the mixture becomes pale. I would recommend using an electric whisk, although you can do it by hand, too. You will need to have the butter at room temperature before you start (see Temperature tips on p. 54 for more details).

Since xylitol is coarser than, say, caster sugar, the beaten mixture won't be particularly fluffy, especially if you compare it with a creamed butter and caster sugar mixture. However, this is nothing to worry about. Usually 3-5 minutes of electric whisking will be sufficient.

Rubbing

When making pastry or crumble you need to rub butter and flour together. Use your fingertips to do this (you can also use a food processor if you wish) and lift your hands at the same time as you rub the flour and butter together. This lets more air into the mixture and helps to make the pastry lighter.

Temperature tips

Eggs used in the recipes should be at room temperature. There is a chance they will curdle if they're cold. So, if you're storing your eggs in a refrigerator, take them out a couple of hours beforehand.

If you need to beat butter and xylitol together, the butter should be at room temperature. Take the butter out of the refrigerator at least an hour in advance. You can help the softening process by cutting it into small cubes.

If you're making pastry or crumble, the butter should be cold.

Heating and boiling milk

Milk can burn easily when heated and lactose-free milk burns even faster. So, bring the milk to the boil slowly on a gentle heat and stir constantly.

If you get melted chocolate all over
your hands, you're eating it too
slowly.
- Author unknown

Melting chocolate

The best way to melt chocolate is to use a heat-proof bowl on top of a saucepan that has some water in it (make sure the water level is not high enough to touch the bowl). If you're not using chocolate drops, chop the chocolate into small pieces and put them into the bowl. Bring the water to the boil in the saucepan, then turn the heat down, place the bowl of chocolate on top of the sauce-pan and let the chocolate melt slowly. Stir occasionally.

Although this method may seem like a lot of effort, it's safer than using a microwave oven. Microwaves can char your chocolate in an instant and spoil your treats, not to mention leave a foul smell behind which is difficult to get rid of and will haunt you for days after-wards (I speak from experience...)

Baking dishes

Use the right size and right kind of baking dish. The recipe will tell you this. Depending on what kind of treat you're baking, it could be either a tin or glass/earthenware dish. If you use, say, a Pyrex dish instead of a tin, your treat is not likely to be ready in the amount of time specified in the recipe. And if you use a tin when you're supposed to use a glass dish, your treat might get burned if you leave it in the oven for as long as the recipe indicates.

It's also important to use the right size baking dish. The recipe will specify this. If you decide to deviate from this, make sure you keep an eye on your treat in the oven more carefully than normally as the cooking time in the recipe may no longer apply accurately.

When baking cakes, you should always fill the tin no more than half full. This will leave room for the cake to rise.

The dish sizes (and other size measures) in the recipes are given in centimetres. If you're used to inches, have a look at the conversion table at the back of the book.

Lining a cake tin

Even if you're using a non-stick tin, it's not worth taking the risk of ending up with a cake that stubbornly refuses to budge. Use non-stick baking paper and cut a piece the shape and size of the bottom of the cake tin. Then cut a piece or pieces that will cover the sides of the tin. Grease the tin with butter or non-dairy vegetable margarine, then place the pieces of non-stick baking paper on the inside of the tin. Greasing will help the baking paper to stay in place.

If you're looking for a more convenient way of doing this, you can buy ready-made cake tin liners and loaf tin liners from some super-markets and cook shops. With these you don't necessarily need to grease your tins.

Ovens

Always pre-heat the oven when you start preparing your treats. The recipe will prompt you to do this. It's important that the cakes and other treats go into a hot oven as soon as you've finished the preparation. It usually takes about 10 minutes for an oven to reach the temperature of 180C/350F/gas mark 4.

Place the treats in the middle of the oven (in fan-assisted ovens this is not so crucial) so that they have the best chance of cooking evenly. Some ovens are warmer at the back, so you may need to turn your treats towards the end to make sure the treats are baked evenly.

Cakes and other treats need a steady temperature in order to rise properly. If you open the door, the oven's temperature will suddenly drop, making the air bubbles inside the cake contract. This will flatten your cake. So, tempting as it may be, try not to open the door until after three quarters of the cooking time at the earliest. If you're making soufflés or other fluffy treats, you really should not open the oven door at all.

All ovens vary, so always treat the cooking time in the recipe as an approximate. Even if you're doing the same recipe again and using the same oven, you'll need to watch out as the cooking time may not be exactly the same the second time around.

It's important to get to know your oven. If you notice that everything cooks quicker than indicated in the recipe, bear this in mind for the future. Generally speaking, fan-assisted ovens can be set about 10-20C/25F/1 gas mark lower than ordinary ovens. However, as with other ovens, they do vary, and I have, for instance, used a fan-assisted one that didn't need any adjusting at all.

Knowing when your cake is baked

When you're using gluten-free flour, it's not so straightforward to determine when the cake is ready. Many gluten-free flour mixes look paler than ordinary wheat flour when baked. Therefore, it's easy to assume that the cake is not cooked even though it is. If you leave gluten-free cakes, pastries or crumbles in the oven for too long, they can become chewy.

Use a metal skewer, or a toothpick, to check whether the cake is ready. Insert it in the middle of the cake: if it comes out dry and nothing sticks to it, it's done. The middle of the cake should also feel 'springy' to touch.

If the top of your cake browns too fast, but the middle remains uncooked, take some non-stick baking paper, cut a piece the size of the cake, make a 2-3 cm hole in the middle and cover the top of the cake with it.

DIY piping bag

If you don't have a piping bag, you can use a plastic food bag instead. Spoon the cream or the sauce you want to pipe into the bag and squeeze it into one of the corners. Cut the corner with a pair of scissors and start piping. It's best to make just a small cut to start with and see how thinly or thickly the cream or sauce is coming out. If you need a bigger hole, make another cut.

A recipe has no soul. You, as the cook, must bring soul to the recipe.

- Thomas Keller

Recipes

People that eat pancakes with jam can't be altogether dangerous.

- Finn Family Moomintroll

Brilliant breakfasts

Gluten-free
Wheat-free
Sugar-free
Yeast-free
Soya-free
Egg-free
Peanut-free
Corn-free
Vegetarian

* Nut-free
* Low lactose

Strawberry boost

Serves 2

This is a superb breakfast. Not only does it taste yummy, but it also keeps the hunger away for a long time. It's an ideal treat for those with high cholesterol as oats and almonds are said to contribute to lowering it.

15 g whole blanched almonds
35 g gluten-free oats
200 g natural yoghurt
200 g strawberries
1 tsp vanilla extract
50 ml apple juice
Sweet Freedom to taste

1. Blitz the almonds and the oats in a food processor or electric chopper.

2. Add the yogurt, strawberries, vanilla extract and apple juice and blitz until the mixture is smooth.

3. Taste and add Sweet Freedom if needed.

4. Pour into glasses and put in a refrigerator for at least 15 minutes. The longer you leave it, the more the oats will swell and the thicker the

mixture will become. If it becomes too thick, just add more apple juice.

* Substitutions

If you can't eat nuts, substitute the almonds for the same amount of oats (so the total amount is 50 g).

To make the treat low in lactose, use natural yogurt with probiotics (bio-cultures).

Try something different

Replace the strawberries with other berries or fruit. For example, blueberries or leftover Poached pears (p. 174) are great alternatives.

Gluten-free
Wheat-free
Sugar-free
Yeast-free
Soya-free
Dairy-free
Casein-free
Lactose-free
Egg-free
Peanut-free
Corn-free
Vegetarian
Vegan

Nut and cranberry bars

Serves 4-6

These nut bars are delightfully crunchy and they will give you lots of energy for the day ahead. It's best to prepare them in advance so that you can just take them from the freezer whenever you want them.

You can buy hazelnut butter in health food shops.

50 g toasted almond flakes
40 g ground almonds
75 g pecan nuts
90 g macadamia nuts
100 g hazelnut butter
60 g dried no-added-sugar cranberries
3 tbsp Sweet Freedom

1. Break the pecan and macadamia nuts into tiny pieces by putting them in a plastic food bag and hammering them with a rolling pin, or blitzing them in an electric chopper for a few seconds. The aim is not to pulverise them, just to chop them into smaller pieces.

2. Line a container suitable for freezing with some cling film or baking paper.

3. Mix all the ingredients together in a bowl. You may find that using your hands will be the easiest way to do this.

4. Press the nut mixture firmly into the container and place in a freezer for at least 4 hours.

5. When you're ready to eat the nut bars, take the container out of the freezer and cut into bars. Serve partly frozen.

What to do with leftovers

Since these nut bars are meant to be kept in the freezer, you don't really have to worry about leftovers. However, you could cut small cubes out of the bars and include them in your Fruit, nut and chocolate platter (p. 120): they taste great with some chocolate drizzled over them.

Gluten-free
Wheat-free
Sugar-free
Yeast-free
Soya-free
Nut-free
Peanut-free
Vegetarian

* Dairy-free
* Casein-free
* Lactose-free

Drop scones

Makes about 20

When you don't have to rush to work in the morning, it's great to indulge a little and make some drop scones for breakfast or brunch.

220 g gluten-free plain white flour
80 g xylitol
2 tsp gluten-free baking powder
a pinch of salt
2 large eggs
120 ml semi-skimmed milk
unsalted butter for frying

1. Mix the flour, xylitol, baking powder and salt in a bowl.

2. Add the eggs and mix.

3. Mix in the milk a little at a time as this will help to get rid of any lumps. Once you have added all the milk, you will notice that the batter is thick.

4. Heat the frying pan on a high heat to start with, then turn to medium heat. Add a knob of butter and spread around the pan. Drop about a tablespoonful of the batter onto it

and fry on both sides. If you have a large pan, you can probably fry up to four drop scones at a time.

* Substitutions

To make these drop scones lactose-free, substitute ordinary milk for Lactofree milk. If you want to make them entirely dairy- and casein-free, use rice or soya drink. In addition, use oil or non-dairy vegetable margarine for frying.

Serving ideas

Serve immediately with the fruit spread of your choice and fresh berries, such as strawberries, blueberries and raspberries. Add a dollop of Vanilla cream (p. 200) or some Custard ice cream (p. 204) if you wish.

Gluten-free
Wheat-free
Sugar-free
Yeast-free
Soya-free
Peanut-free
Vegetarian

* Dairy-free
* Casein-free
* Lactose-free

Pumpkin and rhubarb muffins

Makes 9

The sweetness and earthiness of pumpkin coupled with the zing of rhubarb is just wonderful in these muffins. They also have a streusel topping which makes them look attractive and adds extra texture.

You can buy ready-made pumpkin purée in large supermarkets or health food shops. If you have your own pumpkins, you can use them to make your own purée.

75 g ground almonds
75 g gluten-free plain white flour
175 g xylitol
1 tsp ground cinnamon
½ tsp ground ginger
¼ tsp ground nutmeg
½ tsp bicarbonate of soda
a pinch of salt
1 large egg
120 g pumpkin purée
50 ml vegetable oil
130 g rhubarb

Topping
2 tbsp gluten-free plain white flour
2 tbsp ground almonds
¼ tsp ground cinnamon
30 g unsalted butter

1. Pre-heat the oven to 180C/350F/gas mark 4. Line a muffin tray with 9 paper cases or grease the muffin cups.

2. Make the streusel topping first by putting all of the ingredients in a bowl and rubbing them together with your fingertips. The mixture will become coarse, wet crumble. Place in a refrigerator for the time being.

3. Mix the almonds, flour, xylitol, spices, bicarbonate of soda and salt in a bowl.

4. Chop the rhubarb into tiny pieces.

5. Mix the egg, vegetable oil and pumpkin purée thoroughly in a bowl.

6. Fold in the dry ingredients.

7. Stir in the rhubarb.

8. Spoon the mixture into the muffin cups. Sprinkle the streusel topping on the muffins.

9. Bake for about 30 minutes or until a skewer inserted into a muffin comes out clean.

10. Cool on a wire rack.

* Substitutions

To make the muffins dairy-, casein- and lactose-free, use non-dairy vegetable margarine instead of butter.

Try something different

Instead of rhubarb, try chopped apples, pears or peaches.

One should always eat muffins quite calmly. It is the only way to eat them.
- Oscar Wilde

Gluten-free
Wheat-free
Sugar-free
Yeast-free
Soya-free
Egg-free
Nut-free
Peanut-free
Corn-free
Vegetarian

* Low lactose
* Lactose-free

Creamy strawberry and passion fruit quark

Serves 4-6

This is a refreshing treat that is quick to make. Quark has a high protein content which makes it an ideal ingredient for low carbohydrate diets.

300 ml whipping cream
227 g quark
40-50 g xylitol
2 tsp vanilla extract
250 g strawberries
4 passion fruit

1. Put the cream, xylitol and vanilla extract in a bowl and whisk until soft peaks form.

2. If there is any extra liquid in the quark tub, tip it out. Then stir it into the cream.

3. Cut the strawberries into small pieces and add to the mixture. Spoon into a large serving dish (or small individual ones).

4. Scoop out the soft flesh of 4 passion fruit and spoon on top.

* Substitutions

To reduce the amount of lactose in the recipe, use Lactofree cream instead of ordinary whipping cream. If you want to make it entirely lactose free, try using smooth tofu instead of quark in addition to Lactofree cream. Add extra xylitol if need be.

If you don't want to use xylitol, try Sweet Freedom or no-added-sugar fruit spreads. For example, using some strawberry fruit spread intensifies the strawberry flavour. The colour of the mixture will also become pinker. Make sure you taste the treat when you're preparing it as the sweetness levels of different fruit spreads vary.

Try something different

Instead of using quark, try some Polish *twaróg* (curd cheese). It's a little bit grainier than smooth quark, but it will make a lovely treat nonetheless. You can find *twaróg* in large supermarkets that sell Polish food as well as in Polish food shops.

Coffee granita

Serves 6-8

If you're a coffee lover, this coffee granita will wake you up in the morning. It's like having coffee in an ice crystal form. You will need to prepare it in advance, though, as the freezing process takes quite a few hours.

Granita
500 ml strong coffee (espresso would be ideal)
5-6 tbsp xylitol
1 lemon, zest

Topping
300 ml double cream
¾ tsp vanilla extract
50 g xylitol

1. Grate the lemon zest and put it in a bowl or a jug.

2. Add hot coffee and xylitol. Stir and let the xylitol dissolve. Leave to cool to room temperature.

3. Pour into a plastic freezer container and place in a freezer.

4. After 2 hours, check whether the granita has started to form ice crystals. If so, stir it thoroughly so that the crystals get evenly distributed in the container. Repeat this every half an hour until there is no liquid coffee left.

5. To make the topping, mix all the ingredients and whisk until soft peaks form.

6. To serve, spoon the coffee ice crystals into small serving dishes and top them with some cream.

* Substitutions

To make the treat lactose-free, use Lactofree cream instead of ordinary double cream.

Try something different

For a slightly different citrus flavour, substitute the lemon zest for the zest of an orange.

Gluten-free
Wheat-free
Sugar-free
Yeast-free
Soya-free
Egg-free
Nut-free
Peanut-free
Corn-free
Vegetarian

* Dairy-free
* Casein-free
* Lactose-free
* Vegan

Apricot and oat flat bread

Makes 14 pieces

If you like oats, but don't want to have porridge every morning, try a piece of this flat bread instead – or take it with you to work. It will be most delicious if you use very ripe bananas. If your bananas aren't showing any signs of brown on their skins, add an extra spoonful or two of Sweet Freedom to make the bread sweeter.

30 g pumpkin seeds
30 g sunflower seeds
25 g desiccated coconut
160 g gluten-free oats
100 g dried apricots
2 medium bananas
80 g unsalted butter
3 tbsp Sweet Freedom

1. Pre-heat the oven to 180C/350F/gas mark 4. Line an 18 cm x 23 cm high-sided baking tray with non-stick baking paper.

2. Put the pumpkin seeds, sunflower seeds, coconut and oats in a bowl.

3. Chop the apricots into small pieces and mash the bananas. Mix in with the dry ingredients.

4. Place the butter and Sweet Freedom in a saucepan and heat gently until the butter has melted. Stir occasionally.

5. Pour the butter into the bowl and mix thoroughly.

6. Spoon the mixture onto the baking tray and spread it. Press it firmly with the back of a spoon to smooth the surface.

7. Bake for about 30 minutes until the top looks golden brown.

8. Leave to cool, then cut it into 14 pieces.

* Substitutions

To make the treat vegan, dairy-, lactose- and casein-free, use non-dairy vegetable margarine instead of butter.

Food is an important part of a balanced diet.

- Fran Lebowitz

Lunchbox lovelies

Gluten-free
Wheat-free
Sugar-free
Yeast-free
Soya-free
Peanut-free
Vegetarian

* Dairy-free
* Casein-free
* Lactose-free

Summer berry squares

Makes 16 squares

These are a wonderful addition to the lunch-box as the blueberries, raspberries and lemon zest make the squares a really refreshing snack.

175 g soft unsalted butter at room temperature
200 g xylitol
3 large eggs
100 g ground almonds
150 g fine polenta
2 tsp gluten-free baking powder
1 tsp vanilla extract
200 g blueberries
200 g raspberries
1 lemon, zest

1. Pre-heat the oven to 180C/350F/gas mark 4. Line a 24 cm square cake tin with non-stick baking paper.

2. Grate the lemon zest with a fine grater and set aside.

3. Mix the polenta, ground almonds and baking powder in a bowl.

4. In another bowl, whisk the butter and xylitol with an electric whisk for a few minutes.

5. Add the eggs one by one, whisking thoroughly each time.

6. Fold in the dry ingredients and vanilla extract.

7. Stir in the raspberries, blueberries and lemon zest.

8. Spoon the mixture into the baking tin and level with the back of a spoon.

9. Bake for 30-35 minutes or until the top looks golden and a skewer inserted in the middle comes out clean.

10. Once cool, cut into squares.

* Substitutions

To make the squares dairy-, lactose- and casein-free, use non-dairy vegetable margarine instead of butter.

Gluten-free
Wheat-free
Sugar-free
Yeast-free
Soya-free
Nut-free
Peanut-free
Vegetarian

* Dairy-free
* Casein-free
* Lactose-free

Orange and cranberry mini muffins

Makes about 20

These muffins are very moreish. In addition to being great in lunchboxes, they're ideal as sweet canapés at parties.

You will need a mini muffin tray (fitting 24 muffins in a tray) for baking. A silicone one is easier to use than a metal one as you can just pop the muffins out when they have cooled. If you have a metal one, remember to use muffin cases.

100 g soft unsalted butter at room temperature
40 g gluten-free white bread flour
75 g gluten-free plain white flour
1 tsp gluten-free baking powder
2 large eggs
125 g xylitol
1 orange, zest
50 g dried no-added-sugar cranberries

1. Pre-heat the oven to 200C/400F/gas mark 6. If you are not using a silicone mini muffin tray, line your tray with mini muffin cases.

2. Mix the flours and baking powder in a bowl.

3. In another bowl, whisk the soft butter, eggs, xylitol and orange zest thoroughly, preferably with an electric whisk for a few minutes, so that the mixture becomes smooth and slightly fluffy.

4. Fold in the dry ingredients and the dried cranberries.

5. Spoon the dough into the mini muffin tray, making about 20 muffins. Each muffin will rise, so only fill each case up to about three quarters full.

6. Bake in the oven for about 15 minutes or until the muffins look golden.

7. Leave to cool before removing the muffins from the tray.

* Substitutions

To make the muffins dairy-, casein- and lactose-free, use non-dairy vegetable margarine instead of butter.

Gluten-free
Wheat-free
Sugar-free
Yeast-free
Soya-free
Dairy-free
Casein-free
Lactose-free
Peanut-free
Vegetarian

* Nut-free

Biscotti

Makes about 20

Biscotti are twice-baked dry biscuits from Italy. They are a great snack with your afternoon or morning coffee.

1 large egg
100 g xylitol
½ tsp vanilla extract
65 g fine polenta
65 g gluten-free white bread flour
½ tsp gluten-free baking powder
¼ tsp salt
60 g whole blanched almonds
70 g plain xylitol chocolate drops

1. Pre-heat the oven to 180C/350F/gas mark 4. Line a baking tray with non-stick baking paper.

2. Mix the polenta, flour, baking powder and salt in a bowl.

3. In another bowl, whisk the egg and xylitol with an electric whisk until the volume triples.

4. Mix in the vanilla. Fold in the flour mixture, the almonds and the chocolate drops.

5. Spoon the thick mixture onto the baking tray, forming an oblong that looks like a log. The size should be about 25 cm x 5 cm.

6. Bake for 20-25 minutes until the log is pale brown. Take out of the oven and let it cool for 10 minutes.

7. Reduce the oven temperature to 160C/ 325F/gas mark 3.

8. Cut the oblong into 1 cm slices and turn them on their side. Bake for 10 minutes.

9. Turn the slices to the other side and bake for another 5 minutes.

10. Let the biscotti cool and harden on a wire rack for a couple of hours. If you want them really crispy, leave to stand overnight before serving them or storing them in an airtight container.

* Substitutions

If you can't eat nuts, leave out the almonds.

Gluten-free
Wheat-free
Sugar-free
Yeast-free
Soya-free
Peanut-free
Vegetarian

* Dairy-free
* Casein-free
* Lactose-free

Date and walnut cake

Serves 8-12

This is a classic cake that is simple to make. It's delicious with a cup of tea or coffee.

100 g gluten-free plain white flour
100 g ground almonds
100 g unsalted butter
100 g xylitol
180 g dried dates
70 g chopped walnuts
2 large eggs
1 tsp vanilla extract

1. Pre-heat the oven to 180C/350F/gas mark 4. Line a 900 g loaf tin with non-stick baking paper.

2. Chop the dates and walnuts into small pieces.

3. Put the gluten-free flour, ground almonds and butter in a bowl and rub them together with your fingers until crumbs form (they will feel a little wet).

4. Stir in the xylitol, dates and walnuts.

5. Whisk the eggs with the vanilla extract in a separate bowl for a few minutes until they're pale and fluffy. Fold them into the mixture.

6. Spoon the mixture into the loaf tin and bake for 50-60 minutes until the top of the cake looks golden and a skewer inserted in the middle comes out clean.

7. Cool on a wire rack and cut into slices before serving.

* Substitutions

To make the cake dairy-, lactose- and casein-free, use non-dairy vegetable margarine instead of butter.

Try something different

You can use other dried fruit and nuts instead of dates and walnuts. For example, try these combinations: figs and pecan nuts, apricots and almonds, pears and walnuts, and pineapple and Brazil nuts.

Gluten-free
Wheat-free
Sugar-free
Yeast-free
Soya-free
Egg-free
Nut-free
Peanut-free
Corn-free
Vegetarian

* Dairy-free
* Casein-free
* Lactose-free
* Vegan

Mini mince tarts

Makes about 18

When the days are getting shorter and Christmas is drawing closer, it's time for mince pies. These mini versions are great for nibbling in the office or at Christmas parties.

A silicone mini muffin tray (fitting 24 in a tray) is the best kind for baking these tarts as you can pop them out easily once they have cooled.

Pastry
115 g gluten-free white bread flour
1 tbsp xylitol
50 g unsalted butter
1 orange, zest and 1-3 tsp of juice

Filling
200 g dried fruit (use a mixture of your favourite fruit: choose, for example, from dates, apricots, prunes, sultanas, currants, raisins and figs)
1 orange, zest and juice + the leftover juice from the orange used for the pastry
¾ tsp cinnamon
¼ tsp allspice

1. Start by making the filling. Chop the dried fruit into small pieces and put them together with the spices and the zest and juice of 1 orange into a saucepan.

2. Grate the orange meant for the pastry into a separate bowl, squeeze 3 tsp of its juice into a small dish for later and squeeze the rest of the juice into the saucepan.

3. Cover the saucepan with a lid and simmer on a low heat for 10-15 minutes. Stir occasionally.

4. When the dried fruit have absorbed the juice and softened, take the saucepan off the hob and stir vigorously to make the texture smoother. Set aside to cool while you make the pastry.

5. Pre-heat the oven to 200C/400F/gas mark 6.

6. To make the pastry, place the flour, xylitol, butter and orange zest in a bowl and rub the ingredients together with your fingertips.

7. When the mixture looks and feels like fine crumbs, add half a teaspoon of orange juice and use your fingers to combine it. Keep adding orange juice half a teaspoon at a time until the crumbs stay in a ball.

8. Press the pastry into the moulds of a silicone mini muffin tray. There is enough pastry for about 18 tarts.

9. Fill the cases with the mince.

10. Bake in the oven for about 20 minutes or until the edges of the cases have slightly browned. Remember that gluten-free flour doesn't brown in the same way as normal flour, so your tarts will be paler than ordinary mince pies.

* Substitutions

If you want to make vegan, dairy-, lactose- or casein-free tarts, use non-dairy vegetable margarine instead of butter.

Try something different

Try using different combinations of dried fruit: for example, fig and apricot tarts are quite different from those made with sultanas, raisins and prunes. You can also add chopped nuts, such as hazelnuts or pecan nuts, into the dried fruit mixture or use almond flakes to decorate the tarts.

There is no love sincerer than the love of food.

- George Bernard Shaw

Chocolate almond bites

Makes about 20

These chocolate almond bites are crispy on the outside and lovely and gooey on the inside.

125 g ground almonds
60 g xylitol
35 g plain xylitol chocolate
75 ml double cream
1 tsp vanilla extract
1 large egg white

1. Pre-heat the oven to 160C/325F/gas mark 3. Line 1-2 baking tray(s) with non-stick baking paper. (If your baking trays are small, you will need two.)

2. Put the chocolate, double cream, xylitol and vanilla extract into a heat-proof bowl and balance it over a saucepan which has some water in it. Heat gently to melt the chocolate. Stir occasionally. When the mixture is smooth, remove from the heat.

3. Stir in the almonds.

4. Add the egg white (no need to whisk it first) and mix thoroughly.

5. Make about 20 biscuits by putting heaped teaspoonfuls of dough onto the baking tray(s). You may want to smooth the shape of the biscuits with a palette knife if you like your biscuits less rustic looking. These biscuits won't spread much in the oven, so they will look more or less the same before and after baking.

6. Bake for 10-15 minutes.

7. Take out of the oven and leave to cool on a wire rack.

* Substitutions

If you want to make these bites lactose-free, use Lactofree cream instead of double cream.

Gluten-free
Wheat-free
Sugar-free
Yeast-free
Soya-free
Nut-free
Peanut-free
Vegetarian

* Low lactose

Banana bread

Serves 8-10

This banana bread is not excessively sweet, but it's super yummy nonetheless. It's important that you use ripe bananas as they will make the cake taste better.

250 g gluten-free plain white flour
1 tsp bicarbonate of soda
½ tsp salt
110 g soft unsalted butter at room temperature
200 g xylitol
2 large eggs
4 large ripe bananas
100 ml buttermilk
1 tsp vanilla extract

1. Pre-heat the oven to 180C/350F/gas mark 4. Line a 900 g loaf tin with non-stick baking paper.

2. Mix the flour, bicarbonate of soda and salt in a bowl.

3. Mash the bananas with a fork.

4. Mix the butter and xylitol in another bowl with an electric whisk for a few minutes.

5. Add the eggs into the mixture one at a time, whisking thoroughly each time.

6. Mix in the mashed bananas, buttermilk and vanilla extract.

7. Fold in the flour mixture.

8. Spoon the mixture into the loaf tin and bake for about an hour or until the top looks golden brown and a skewer inserted into the middle comes out clean.

9. Take out of the oven and let the loaf cool for about five minutes before taking it out of the tin and placing it on a wire rack to cool. Serve while it's still slightly warm.

* Substitutions

Substitute butter for non-dairy vegetable margarine and buttermilk for Polish *kefir* (a fermented milk drink) with probiotics to make this treat low in lactose. You can buy *kefir* in Polish shops or large supermarkets.

One of the very nicest things about life is the way we must regularly stop whatever it is we are doing and devote our attention to eating.
- Luciano Pavarotti

Afternoon indulgencies

Lemon cheesecake

Serves 8-10

This cheesecake has a pastry base. If the idea of making pastry makes you anxious, I can assure you that there's no need to worry. Instead of rolling the pastry, you can just press it with your fingers onto the bottom of the baking tin. Because of the gluten-free flour, the end result will be naturally light and delightfully crumbly.

Base
40 g gluten-free white bread flour
40 g gluten-free plain white flour
40 g unsalted butter
30 g xylitol
1-3 tsp lemon juice (taken from the juice for the lemon glazing)

Cheese filling
200 g cream cheese (for example, Philadelphia)
200 ml double cream
100 g xylitol
2 tsp vanilla extract
2 lemons, zest

Lemon glazing
2 lemons, juice (minus what is needed for the base)
150 ml water
50 g xylitol
1 tbsp corn flour

1. Line a 20 cm round spring-form baking tin with non-stick baking paper.

2. Start by grating 2 lemons and putting the zest into a large mixing bowl. Squeeze the lemon juice into a saucepan.

3. Then make the base. Rub the flours and the butter into a crumble with your fingertips. Mix in the xylitol. Take 1 tsp of lemon juice from the saucepan and add to the crumble. Use your fingers to combine it into a ball. Add more lemon juice if needed, half a teaspoon at a time.

4. Press the pastry to the bottom of the baking tin. Place in a refrigerator while you heat the oven to 190C/375F/gas mark 5. When the oven is up to temperature, bake the pastry for about 20 minutes or until thoroughly cooked. Remember that gluten-free flour won't brown in the same way as ordinary wheat flour. Take out of the oven and put aside to cool.

5. To make the lemon glazing, add water, xylitol and corn flour into the saucepan which already has the lemon juice in it. Whisk well. Put the saucepan on a medium heat and stir until the sauce comes to the boil and begins to thicken. Continue stirring for 2-3 minutes. Take off the heat and leave aside to cool.

6. To make the cheese filling, stir together the cream cheese and the lemon zest in a bowl. In a separate bowl, whisk the cream with xylitol and vanilla extract until soft peaks form. Add this to the cream cheese mixture and stir thoroughly.

7. When the base has cooled, spoon the cheese filling into the baking tin and smooth the surface with a palette knife. Spread the lemon glazing on top using a clean palette knife.

8. Place the cake in a refrigerator to cool for at least a couple of hours before serving.

* Substitutions

To make this cheesecake lactose-free, use non-dairy vegetable margarine instead of butter, Lactofree cream instead of ordinary cream and the Lactofree variety of cream cheese ('Soft White Cheese').

Cheesecake packs a sensual wallop unlike anything in the natural world because it is a brew of megadoses of agreeable stimuli which we concocted for the express purpose of pressing our pleasure buttons.
- Steven Pinker

Gluten-free
Wheat-free
Sugar-free
Yeast-free
Soya-free
Peanut-free
Corn-free
Vegetarian

* Lactose-free

Heavenly chocolate cake

Serves 6-8

This is my favourite chocolate cake of all times. It's simply heavenly. I often make it when we have guests as it never lets me, or the guests, down.

Cake
100 g plain xylitol chocolate
150 ml double cream
75 g xylitol
3 large eggs
50 g ground almonds
1 tsp vanilla extract

Topping
100 ml double cream
75 g xylitol
100 g plain xylitol chocolate
1 tsp vanilla extract

1. Pre-heat the oven to 160C/325F/gas mark 3. Line a 20 cm round spring-form cake tin with non-stick baking paper.

2. Put the chocolate for the cake in a heat-proof bowl together with the cream, vanilla extract and 50 g of xylitol. Balance the bowl over a saucepan which has some water in it. Heat gently to melt the chocolate. Stir occasionally.

3. When the mixture is smooth, take the bowl off the saucepan and stir in the ground almonds. Set aside.

4. Take another bowl and whisk the eggs and 25 g of xylitol with an electric whisk until their volume has tripled.

5. Fold the whisked eggs and xylitol into the chocolate mixture. Use a metal spoon.

6. Pour the cake mixture into the baking tin and put it in the oven for about 25 minutes.

7. Meanwhile, make the topping. Put all the ingredients in a heat-proof bowl. Balance the bowl over a saucepan which has some water in it and heat gently. Stir occasionally.

8. When the mixture is smooth, take the bowl off the saucepan and set aside to cool at room temperature.

9. When the cake is ready, take it from the oven and let it cool in the tin.

10. After the cake has cooled, place it on a serving plate and spread the topping over it. The topping will set better if you put the cake in a refrigerator for an hour or two.

* Substitutions

If you want to make this cake lactose-free, use Lactofree cream instead of ordinary double cream.

Serving ideas

Serve on its own or with Vanilla cream (p. 200) and raspberries.

Try something different

If you prefer your chocolate cake less dark, use xylitol-sweetened No Added Sugar Alternative to Milk Chocolate or fructose-sweetened milk chocolate instead of plain xylitol chocolate (see pp. 40-41 for more details).

Chocolate is the answer. Who cares
what the question is.
- Author unknown

Torta de banana

Serves 7-9

This is an upside down cake. The delicious combination of the soft and sweet banana and the tangy lime is guaranteed to make your guests reach for a second slice.

4 ripe bananas
180 g xylitol
175 g soft unsalted butter at room temperature
2 large eggs
2 limes, zest and juice
150 g gluten-free plain white flour
1 tsp gluten-free baking powder

1. Pre-heat the oven to 180C/350F/gas mark 4. Line a 20 cm round spring-form baking tin with non-stick baking paper.

2. Peel and slice the bananas. Put the slices at the bottom of the baking tin.

3. Grate the limes and put the zest in a small bowl for the time being. Squeeze the juice of 1 lime into the same bowl and the other onto the bananas.

4. Mix the flour and the baking powder in another bowl and set aside.

5. Take yet another bowl and whisk the butter and the xylitol with an electric whisk for a few minutes.

6. Add the eggs one by one, whisking all the time. Once the mixture looks smooth again, mix in the lime juice and zest. Fold in the flour.

7. Spoon the dough into the baking tin on top of the bananas and smooth the top. Bake for 40-50 minutes or until the cake looks golden and a skewer inserted in the middle comes out clean.

8. Let the cake stand for a while to cool. Then turn it upside down onto a serving plate. Best served slightly warm.

* Substitutions

To make the cake dairy-, casein- and lactose-free, substitute butter for non-dairy vegetable margarine.

Gluten-free
Wheat-free
Sugar-free
Yeast-free
Soya-free
Nut-free
Peanut-free
Vegetarian

* Low lactose

Apple and custard tart

Serves 10-12

I have modified this tart from my mum's yummy recipe. Although there are several stages in the preparation process, they're worth the time.

Base
100 g soft unsalted butter at room temperature
100 g xylitol
1 large egg
150 g fine polenta
80 g gluten-free plain white flour
1 tsp gluten-free baking powder

Apple filling
7 Cox's apples
1 tbsp lemon juice

Custard filling
450 g Greek yogurt
2 large eggs
100 g xylitol
2 tbsp corn flour
2 tsp vanilla extract

Decorative topping
1-2 Cox's apples
1 tbsp xylitol

1. Whisk the soft butter and xylitol with an electric whisk for a couple of minutes. Add the egg and whisk thoroughly.

2. Mix in the polenta, gluten-free flour and baking powder. It's best to use your hands since the dough will be thick. Place the dough in a refrigerator while you make the apple filling.

3. Peel, core and chop 7 apples into small pieces and put them into a saucepan. Add the lemon juice. Simmer over a gentle heat under a lid for about 10 minutes, or until the apples are soft. Take the saucepan off the heat and purée the apple pieces. If the apples are soft enough, the back of a spoon will do the job. Set aside to cool.

4. Pre-heat the oven to 180C/350F/gas mark 4. Line a 23 cm round spring-form baking tin with non-stick baking paper.

5. Press the dough on the bottom and sides of the tin with your fingers. The sides need to be quite high (6-7 cm). If the dough sticks to your fingers, sprinkle a little gluten-free flour on it.

Put the tin in the refrigerator for the time being.

6. To make the custard filling, mix all the ingredients together with a whisk.

7. Take the baking tin from the refrigerator and spoon the apple filling into it. Smooth the surface with the back of a spoon. Add the custard filling and smooth it as well.

8. To make the decorative topping, quarter and core the apples. I usually leave the skin on. However, if you prefer to peel your apples, that's fine, too. Slice the quarters into thin wedges and place them on top of the custard filling. Sprinkle xylitol on top and bake in the oven for about 45 minutes.

* Substitutions

To make the tart low in lactose, use non-dairy vegetable margarine instead of butter and Greek yogurt with probiotics (bio-cultures).

Try something different

Instead of apple, try using rhubarb.

Life is an apple. Take a big bite.
- Fricafresh

Gluten-free
Wheat-free
Sugar-free
Yeast-free
Soya-free
Peanut-free
Corn-free
Vegetarian

* Lactose-free

Coffee and pecan cake

Serves 10-12

This is one of those 'melt in your mouth' kind of cakes. It's rich and moreish at the same time.

Cake
230 g pecan halves (200 g for grinding + 30 g for decoration)
2 tbsp instant coffee powder
7 large eggs
200 g xylitol
a pinch of salt

Filling
500 ml double cream
1 tbsp instant coffee powder
1 tsp vanilla extract
50 g xylitol

1. Pre-heat the oven to 180C/350F/gas mark 4. Line two 23 cm round cake tins with non-stick baking paper.

2. Start by making the cake batter. Grind 200 g of the pecan halves as finely as possible in an electric chopper or food processor. Make sure you leave 30 g of unbroken pecan halves for decoration.

3. Separate the eggs and put the yolks into one bowl and the whites into another.

4. Add a pinch of salt to the egg whites and whisk with an electric whisk until they become so stiff that you can turn the bowl upside down and they won't drop. Set aside.

5. Sieve the instant coffee powder into the egg yolk bowl and add the xylitol. Whisk with an electric whisk for a few minutes until the mixture becomes pale and fluffy.

6. Fold the ground pecan nuts into the egg yolk mixture.

7. Fold in the egg whites, a little at a time, with a metal spoon.

8. Pour the mixture into the two baking tins, smooth the tops with the back of a spoon and bake in the oven for 25-30 minutes.

9. While the cakes are in the oven, prepare the coffee cream filling. Pour the cream into a large bowl and add the xylitol and vanilla

extract. Sieve the instant coffee powder into the bowl, too, and whisk until soft peaks form. Place in a refrigerator to keep cool.

10. Take the cakes out of the oven when a skewer inserted in the middle comes out clean. Let them cool to room temperature.

11. To assemble, place one of the cakes on a serving plate. If it looks like the top surface is uneven, cut any excess off with a sharp knife. Then spread about a third of the coffee cream onto it. Place the other cake on top and use the rest of the coffee cream to cover the whole cake. You can use a palette knife or the back of a spoon to do this.

12. Decorate with pecan halves. Place in a refrigerator for a couple of hours before serving.

* Substitutions

To make the cake lactose-free, substitute double cream for Lactofree cream.

Coffee smells like freshly ground
heaven.

- Jessi Lane Adams

Gluten-free
Wheat-free
Sugar-free
Yeast-free
Soya-free
Egg-free
Peanut-free
Corn-free
Vegetarian

* Lactose-free

Fruit, nut and chocolate platter

Serves 4-6

Dried fruit and nuts drizzled with chocolate make delightful afternoon nibbles, and what is more, this impressive-looking platter is quick and simple to prepare.

10 dried apricots
10 dried figs
10 dried dates (preferably medjool dates)
10-20 whole blanched almonds
10-20 pecan nuts
10-20 walnuts

Chocolate sauce
60 g plain xylitol chocolate
70 ml double cream
½ tsp vanilla extract
1 ½ tbsp xylitol

1. Start by making the chocolate sauce. Put all the ingredients into a saucepan. Heat gently and stir continuously until the chocolate has melted and the sauce has thickened. Set aside while you prepare the fruit and nuts.

2. Make a 'pocket' into each dried fruit by cutting them from one end to the other, but without actually cutting the fruit completely into half. Making the cut on the top side will show the nuts better and the platter will look more attractive.

3. Fill each apricot with 1-2 almonds, each fig with 1-2 pecan nuts and each date with 1-2 walnuts. The size of your dried fruit will determine how many nuts you can fit inside them.

4. Place them on a serving platter and pipe the chocolate sauce over them.

5. Refrigerate for a couple of hours to allow the chocolate to set.

* Substitutions

To make these nibbles lactose-free, substitute ordinary cream for Lactofree cream.

Gluten-free
Wheat-free
Sugar-free
Yeast-free
Soya-free
Nut-free
Peanut-free
Vegetarian

* Lactose-free

Chocolate and vanilla celebration cake

Serves 6-8

This is a light chocolate sponge covered with vanilla loveliness and grated chocolate. It's an irresistible cake for celebrating anything and everything.

Cake
4 large eggs
20 g gluten-free plain white flour
20 g gluten-free white bread flour
20 g cocoa powder
¼ tsp salt
110 g xylitol
½ tsp vanilla extract

Topping
250 ml whipping cream
1 tsp vanilla extract
25 g xylitol
50 g plain xylitol chocolate

1. Pre-heat the oven to 180C/350F/gas mark 4. Line a 20 cm round spring-form cake tin with non-stick baking paper. Put the chocolate in a refrigerator.

2. Separate the yolks and whites of 3 eggs into separate bowls.

3. Add the fourth egg, salt, xylitol and vanilla extract to the yolks and mix thoroughly. Then sieve and add the flour and cocoa powder. Whisk for a couple of minutes until the mixture is light and fluffy.

4. Whisk the egg whites with an electric whisk until they become so stiff that you can turn the bowl upside down and they won't drop. (Remember to use a clean whisk, otherwise the whites won't stiffen.)

5. Fold in the egg whites with a metal spoon. Start by folding in a few spoonfuls before tipping in the rest.

6. Pour the mixture into the baking tin and bake for about 30 minutes or until a skewer inserted in the middle of the cake comes out clean.

7. Leave the cake to cool in the tin.

Cake is happiness! If you know the way of the cake, you know the way of happiness! If you have a cake in front of you, you should not look any further for joy!
- C. JoyBell C.

8. When the cake has cooled, make the topping. Whisk the cream, xylitol and vanilla until soft peaks form.

9. Spread the cream over the top and the sides of the cake with a palette knife or the back of a spoon.

10. Take the chocolate out of the refrigerator, grate it and sprinkle over the cake.

* Substitutions

You can make this cake lactose-free by using Lactofree cream instead of ordinary whipping cream.

Try something different

You can also use a 'milkier' variety of chocolate if you don't fancy dark chocolate. Try xylitol-sweetened No Added Sugar Alternative to Milk Chocolate or fructose-sweetened milk chocolate (see pp. 40-41 for more details).

Life is uncertain. Eat dessert first.

- Ernestine Ulmer

Delicious desserts

Gluten-free
Wheat-free
Sugar-free
Yeast-free
Soya-free
Nut-free
Peanut-free
Corn-free
Vegetarian

* Lactose-free

Milk chocolate mousse

Serves 6

This chocolate mousse melts in your mouth and it's a great way to finish off a meal.

100 g plain xylitol chocolate
2 large eggs
300 ml double cream
70 g xylitol
1 tsp vanilla extract

1. Put the chocolate into a heat-proof bowl and balance it over a saucepan that has some water in it. Heat gently to melt the chocolate. Stir occasionally. When the chocolate has melted, take off the heat and set aside.

2. Separate the egg whites from the yolks and put them in two different bowls.

3. Whisk the egg yolks with 50 g of xylitol until fluffy and pale. Add the melted chocolate and mix well. Set aside.

4. Whisk the cream, 20 g of xylitol and vanilla extract until soft peaks form.

5. Combine with the chocolate and egg yolk mixture. Set aside.

6. Whisk the egg whites with an electric whisk until firm. You will know when you've whisked enough by turning the bowl upside down: the egg whites should stay in the bowl and not drop.

7. Gently fold a little of the whisked egg white into the chocolate cream mixture with a metal spoon, then fold in the rest.

8. Spoon into 6 ramekins and chill in a refrigerator for at least a couple of hours before serving.

* Substitutions

To make the mousse lactose-free, substitute double cream for Lactofree cream.

What to do with leftovers

You can freeze any leftover portions. In fact, you can even serve them partly frozen, like chocolate ice cream.

Gluten-free
Wheat-free
Sugar-free
Yeast-free
Soya-free
Nut-free
Peanut-free
Vegetarian

* Lactose-free

Profiteroles

Makes 18-20

To make profiteroles successfully, you will need to make them quickly. Therefore, you need to get all the preparation done first. Also, profiteroles go soggy quickly, so put the cream filling and the chocolate sauce on top just before serving.

Profiteroles
150 ml cold water
50 g unsalted butter
85 g gluten-free plain white flour
2 tsp xylitol
2 large eggs

Cream filling
240 ml whipping cream
1 tsp vanilla extract
45 g xylitol

Chocolate sauce
50 g plain xylitol chocolate
60 ml double cream
½ tsp vanilla extract
1 tbsp xylitol

1. Pre-heat the oven to 200C/400F/gas mark 6.

2. Cut a piece of non-stick baking paper to fit the size of your baking tray, wet it under cold running water for a couple of seconds and place it on the tray.

3. Sift the flour through a sieve and put it in a bowl with the xylitol. Set aside.

4. Put the eggs into a glass or a small measuring jug and beat them with a fork until thoroughly mixed. Set aside.

5. Measure the cold water and the butter and put them into a saucepan. Bring to the boil over a moderate heat, stirring every now and then.

6. As soon as the water starts to boil, take off the heat and beat in the flour and xylitol mixture. Keep on beating vigorously until a smooth ball of paste forms and leaves the sides of the saucepan.

7. Add the egg a little at a time, each time beating it until the paste is thoroughly combined. The end result will be a smooth and glossy paste.

8. Use a teaspoon to make 18-20 dollops on a baking tray.

9. Bake for 10 minutes, then increase the oven temperature to 220C/425F/gas mark 7, and bake for another 5-10 minutes. When the profiteroles are golden and crisp, take them out of the oven.

10. Pierce the side of each profiterole with a toothpick or skewer to let the steam out and place them on a wire rack to cool.

11. While they are cooling, prepare the cream filling: whisk all the ingredients in a bowl until firm peaks form. Place the bowl in a refrigerator for the time being.

12. To make the chocolate sauce, put all the ingredients in a saucepan and heat gently. Stir all the time until the chocolate melts and the mixture thickens. Set aside.

13. To assemble the dessert, take each profiterole and cut horizontally into halves. Spread a heaped teaspoonful of cream on the bottom and gently press the top onto it. Place the profiteroles on a serving plate or bowl.

14. Use a piping bag or a spoon to spread the chocolate sauce over the profiteroles. Serve immediately.

* Substitutions

To make the profiteroles lactose-free, use non-dairy vegetable margarine instead of butter and Lactofree cream instead of ordinary cream.

Serving ideas

Although profiteroles make a yummy dessert, you can also serve them as sweet canapés at a party. Just put the profiteroles on a serving tray and pipe the chocolate sauce on them.

Try something different

Make a double portion of Milk chocolate mousse (p. 128) and place it at the bottom of a large serving dish which has high sides. Build a tower of profiteroles on top of it and use a piping bag to drizzle the chocolate sauce on top. This will make an impressive looking dessert for special occasions.

Grilled pineapple with pistachio ice cream

Serves 4

You will need to prepare the pistachio ice cream at least a day before you're planning to serve this dessert. If you have guests coming for dinner, this is an advantage as you can make most of the preparations in advance and don't need get stressed at the last minute.

Pistachio ice cream
400 ml double cream
50 g xylitol
1 ¼ tsp vanilla extract
2 large egg yolks
50 g pistachio nuts

Grilled pineapple
1 medium ripe pineapple
6 tbsp Sweet Freedom
¾ tsp ground cinnamon

1. Start by making the pistachio ice cream: separate the egg whites from the yolks and put the yolks in a large wide-necked jug.

2. Chop the pistachio nuts into tiny pieces and set aside. If you want to use an electric chopper, make sure you don't pulverise the nuts completely. A little bit of crunchiness is nice in the ice cream.

3. Place the cream, xylitol and vanilla extract in a saucepan and bring to the boil over a gentle heat. Stir constantly with a whisk.

4. When the mixture starts to boil, take off the heat and pour slowly into the jug containing the egg yolks and whisk continuously.

5. Mix in the chopped pistachio nuts.

6. Pour the mixture into a container that is suitable for freezing and leave to cool to room temperature. When the mixture has cooled, place the container in a freezer. Leave to freeze overnight.

7. When you're ready to make the grilled pineapple, take the ice cream from the freezer so that it can soften a little before serving.

8. Peel the pineapple and cut it into 1 cm slices. Cut out the core.

Ice cream is happiness condensed.

- Jessi Lane Adams

9. Mix Sweet Freedom and cinnamon in a bowl.

10. Dunk the pineapple slices into the Sweet Freedom to coat them lightly.

11. Grill them on a griddle pan until both sides are golden brown. Take care not to burn them. Serve straightaway with the ice cream.

* Substitutions

To make this treat lactose-free, use Lactofree cream instead of double cream. However, because the fat content of the Lactofree cream is lower than that of double cream, it's more prone to developing ice crystals. Therefore, you should stir the ice cream every 1-2 hours during the freezing process.

If you don't eat any dairy at all, you can serve the grilled pineapple without the pistachio ice cream.

Gluten-free
Wheat-free
Sugar-free
Yeast-free
Soya-free
Dairy-free
Casein-free
Lactose-free
Peanut-free
Corn-free
Vegetarian

Apple cake

Serves 8-10

If you want some comfort food for pudding, this apple cake is it. It's lovely and moist – and a perfect way to use any spare apples.

The amount of xylitol needed in the cake depends on the variety of apples you have. If you're using a very sweet variety, you will need a smaller amount of sweetener than if you're using a tarter variety.

Apple purée
3 large eating apples
2 tbsp lemon juice
1 tbsp xylitol

Cake
4 large eggs
160 g ground almonds
125-150 g xylitol
2 tbsp lemon juice
25 g flaked almonds for decoration

1. Start by making the apple purée: peel, core and chop the apples into small chunks and place in a saucepan with the lemon juice and xylitol. Simmer gently under a lid for

10-15 minutes, or until the apples have softened. Mash the apple into a purée and set aside to cool.

2. Pre-heat the oven to 180C/350F/gas mark 4. Line a 20 cm round spring-form baking tin with non-stick baking paper.

3. Whisk the eggs and the xylitol until pale and fluffy.

4. Fold in the ground almonds, apple purée and lemon juice.

5. Spoon into the baking tin and smooth the surface with the back of a spoon. Sprinkle flaked almonds over the top.

6. Bake for 30-35 minutes or until a skewer inserted in the middle of the cake comes out clean.

Serving ideas

Serve hot or cold, with Cinnamon cream (p. 201), Cinnamon ice cream (p. 206) or Custard (p. 202).

Mango fool

Serves 4-6

This is a quick and easy dessert. And it's deliciously creamy and luxurious. Just make sure that the mango you're using is ripe and juicy.

1 large ripe mango
200 g Greek yogurt
300 ml whipping cream
1 lime, juice
Sweet Freedom to taste

1. Peel and chop the mango, squeeze the juice out of the lime and blitz them thoroughly in an electric chopper, blender or food processor.

2. Whisk the cream until soft peaks form.

3. Mix all the ingredients together, apart from the Sweet Freedom. Taste and add a squeeze or two of the sweetener if need be.

4. Put in a refrigerator for at least 15 minutes before serving.

* Substitutions

To reduce the amount of lactose in the recipe, use Greek yogurt with probiotics (bio-cultures) and Lactofree cream instead of ordinary whipping cream.

Serving ideas

Serve cold. If you want to add more fruit and like having 'bits' in your fool, chop another large and juicy mango into small pieces and mix in.

Lemon delicious

Serves 4-5

My Australian friend Bill Sampson introduced me to this delightful dessert. It's wonderfully refreshing and has a fluffy top and a gooey bottom. This is an adaptation of Bill's recipe.

5 large eggs
100 g xylitol
2 lemons, juice and zest
1 ½ tsp corn flour

1. Pre-heat the oven to 160C/325F/gas mark 3. Get two oven-proof dishes ready: one is for baking the pudding in and needs to have at least 5 cm sides; the other should be bigger and also have high sides because the small dish as well as some water will be placed inside it. I usually use a Pyrex or earthenware dish and place it inside a high-sided roasting tray.

2. Grate the lemon zest and squeeze the juices into a small bowl and set aside.

3. Separate the egg yolks from the whites and put them into separate bowls.

4. Whisk the egg whites with an electric whisk until they become so stiff that you can turn the bowl upside down without them dropping. Set aside.

5. Fill a kettle with water and start boiling it. Then continue making the pudding.

6. Add the xylitol and corn flour to the egg yolks and whisk with an electric whisk for a couple of minutes until the mixture becomes creamy.

7. Mix in the lemon zest and juice.

8. Carefully fold in the egg whites a little at a time. Use a metal spoon.

9. Pour the mixture into the baking dish and place it inside the larger dish. Put the dishes in the oven and pour the boiling water into the larger dish so that it is a little over half filled with water. This technique ensures that the pudding will have two layers: the top will be fluffy and the bottom layer will resemble lemon curd.

10. Bake for 20-25 minutes, until the top is lightly golden.

11. Set aside to cool before serving. (The pudding will shrink a little while cooling.) Serve warm or cold.

Serving ideas

If you'd like to add a smooth contrast to the sharpness of the lemon flavour, serve with Vanilla cream (p. 200).

What to do
with leftovers

You can make superb lemon and custard ice cream by following the Custard ice cream recipe (p. 204): just stir the leftover Lemon delicious in with the ice cream mixture once it has reached room temperature and put it in a freezer.

When life hands you a lemon, say,
"Oh yeah, I like lemons! What else
ya got?"
- Henry Rollins

Gluten-free
Wheat-free
Sugar-free
Yeast-free
Soya-free
Nut-free
Peanut-free
Vegetarian

* Lactose-free

Tiramisu
Serves 10-12

This tiramisu has a soft chocolate sponge that is moistened with strong coffee and layered with lemony mascarpone. It's simply blissful.

Chocolate sponge
4 large eggs
150 g xylitol
50 g gluten-free plain white flour
20 g cocoa powder
1 tsp gluten-free baking powder

Coffee for moistening the sponge
150 ml boiling water
1 tbsp instant coffee granules

Mascarpone filling
250 g mascarpone
1 large egg
110 g xylitol
200 ml double cream
1 lemon, zest

Decoration
½-1 tbsp cocoa powder

1. Pre-heat the oven to 190C/375F/gas mark 5. Line a 20-23 cm round or square cake tin with non-stick baking paper. Use a tin that is closest to the shape and size of a high-sided serving dish you're planning to use for serving the tiramisu.

2. To make the sponge, whisk the eggs and the xylitol together with an electric whisk until they become pale and fluffy.

3. Sieve and fold in the flour, cocoa powder and baking powder.

4. Pour into the baking tin and bake for 30-35 minutes or until a skewer inserted into the middle of the cake comes out clean.

5. While the cake is in the oven, make the coffee for moistening the sponge: mix the coffee granules with boiling water and set aside to cool. (You can also use 150 ml of strong filter coffee or espresso.)

6. To make the mascarpone filling, start by whisking the egg and xylitol with an electric whisk until pale and fluffy.

7. Add mascarpone and grated lemon zest and mix thoroughly. Set aside.

8. Whisk the cream in another bowl until soft peaks form.

9. Add to the mascarpone mixture and stir. Place in a refrigerator until you are ready to assemble the dessert.

10. When the sponge has cooled, take a high-sided serving dish and cut pieces of the cake and layer them at the bottom. (If you're using a serving dish that's the same shape and size as your baking tin, you can just cut the cake into two horizontally. If not, the 'patch work' approach will work just as well.) Since there will be two sponge layers, use up to half of the cake for the first layer.

11. To moisten the sponge, spoon half of the strong coffee over it.

12. Spoon half of the mascarpone filling over the sponge and spread evenly.

13. Add the second layer of the sponge, moisten with the remaining coffee and spread the rest of the mascarpone filling on top.

14. Place in a refrigerator until you're ready to serve. Ideally, you should let the tiramisu stand for a few hours.

15. Sieve some cocoa powder on top of the dessert just before serving.

* Substitutions

To make this tiramisu lactose-free, use Lactofree Soft White Cheese instead of mascarpone and Lactofree cream instead of ordinary double cream.

Food is not about impressing people.
It's about making them feel
comfortable.
- Ina Garten

Sumptuous suppers

Gluten-free
Wheat-free
Sugar-free
Yeast-free
Soya-free
Nut-free
Peanut-free
Vegetarian

* Dairy-free
* Casein-free
* Lactose-free

Pancakes

Makes 12-14 pancakes

Pancakes are not only great on Pancake Day – they're yummy at any time of the year. I absolutely love making them for supper, and sometimes when I really want to indulge myself, I skip dinner and just have pancakes...

150 g gluten-free plain white flour
2 large eggs
2 tbsp xylitol
275 ml milk
2 tbsp melted unsalted butter + extra for frying

1. Put the flour and xylitol into a bowl.

2. Add the eggs and mix.

3. Add the milk a little at a time and whisk.

4. Add the melted butter and whisk until the batter is smooth and there are no lumps in it.

5. Fry the pancakes in a small ordinary frying pan or a special pancake frying pan. Heat the pan on a high heat to start with, then turn it down to medium. Grease the pan with a little butter. Spoon about 2 tbsp of the batter into

the pan and tip it around so that the batter covers the bottom of the pan. Fry until the pancake acquires a golden brown marbled look on the bottom side. Turn it over and fry the other side.

6. Fry the rest of the pancakes. Remember to grease the pan with a little butter in between each pancake.

* Substitutions

To make the pancakes lactose-free, use Lactofree milk instead of ordinary milk and non-dairy vegetable margarine or oil instead of butter.

To make the pancakes completely dairy- and casein-free, use rice or soya drink and non-dairy vegetable margarine or oil.

Serving ideas

The traditional way of serving pancakes is with a sprinkling of sugar and a squeeze of lemon, so try using either xylitol or Sweet Freedom as a substitute for sugar. You can also try them with different fruit spreads, fresh berries and Custard ice cream (p. 204) or Cinnamon ice cream (p. 206).

Gluten-free
Wheat-free
Sugar-free
Yeast-free
Soya-free
Egg-free
Nut-free
Peanut-free
Corn-free
Vegetarian

Coconut and chocolate truffles

Makes 15-17

If you fancy decadent nibbles for your supper, try these truffles. They're irresistible.

60 g plain xylitol chocolate
60 g unsalted butter
2 tbsp xylitol
¼ tsp vanilla extract
85 g extra thick double cream
30 g desiccated coconut

1. Put the chocolate, butter, xylitol and vanilla extract into a saucepan. Heat gently and stir constantly until the chocolate and butter have melted, the xylitol has dissolved and the mixture has become smooth and thickened a little. Be careful not to boil it.

2. Take off the heat and add the cream. Stir until the mixture is smooth.

3. Pour into a small bowl and chill in a refrigerator for 8 hours.

4. Put the desiccated coconut into a small bowl.

5. Make small balls out of the hardened chocolate mixture. You can use, for example, a melon scoop or a teaspoon to help you, or you can just use your fingers. Be aware that if you handle the mixture too much, it will melt into your hands. If this happens, place the bowl back in a refrigerator.

6. Roll the truffle balls in the desiccated coconut and place on a serving plate. Store in a refrigerator.

Try something different

You can also use chopped hazelnut nuts, crushed toasted almond flakes or cocoa powder to coat the truffles.

Gluten-free
Wheat-free
Sugar-free
Yeast-free
Soya-free
Dairy-free
Casein-free
Lactose-free
Egg-free
Nut-free
Peanut-free
Corn-free
Fat-free
Vegetarian
Vegan

Apple and mango jelly
Serves 4-5

If you only want a light snack for supper, this jelly is ideal. Because the recipe uses agar flakes instead of gelatine, it's also suitable for vegans.

1 litre apple and mango fruit juice
5 tbsp agar flakes

1. Put the juice into a saucepan and sprinkle the agar flakes over the top. Bring to the boil over a gentle heat, stirring occasionally. The agar flakes will dissolve gradually.

2. Once boiling, simmer for 4 minutes, stirring every now and then.

3. Pour the liquid into individual serving dishes. Cool first to room temperature before placing the dishes in a refrigerator for 3-4 hours.

Try something different

If you want to turn this jelly into something more festive, use it for making an apple and mango jelly trifle:

1. Cut pieces of Apple cake (p. 138) and layer them at the bottom of a high-sided serving dish.

2. Add a layer of sliced mangos.

3. Pour the jelly mixture over them and allow the jelly to set.

4. Add a layer of Custard (p. 202).

5. Add a layer of Vanilla cream (p. 200).

6. Decorate with mango slices.

Lemon loaf

Serves 8-12

This is a summery cake with a subtle lemon flavour.

175 g soft unsalted butter at room temperature
200 g xylitol
3 large eggs
100 g ground almonds
150 g fine polenta
2 tsp gluten-free baking powder
1 tsp vanilla extract
2 lemons, zest

1. Pre-heat the oven to 180C/350F/gas mark 4. Line a 900 g loaf tin with non-stick baking paper.

2. Mix the polenta, ground almonds and baking powder in a bowl and set aside.

3. Grate the lemon zest into a small bowl and set aside.

4. Put the butter and xylitol into a bowl and whisk with an electric whisk for a few minutes.

5. Whisk in the eggs one by one.

6. Fold in the vanilla extract, lemon zest and the dry ingredients.

7. Spoon the dough into the tin and level with the back of a spoon.

8. Bake for 40-45 minutes or until the cake looks golden and a skewer inserted into the centre comes out clean.

9. Remove the cake from the oven and let it cool before taking it out of the tin.

* Substitutions

You can make this cake dairy-, casein- and lactose-free by substituting butter for non-dairy vegetable margarine.

Serving ideas

Although you can serve slices of this loaf on their own, you can make your supper a little bit more special by serving it with Vanilla cream (p. 200) and raspberries.

Gluten-free
Wheat-free
Sugar-free
Yeast-free
Soya-free
Dairy-free
Casein-free
Lactose-free
Peanut-free
Vegetarian

* Nut-free

Chocolate brownies

Makes 16 squares

These brownies are rich, gooey, a little bit crunchy and suitably decadent. If you happen to have any left over from your supper, take a square or two to work the following day – it will light up your day (and make your colleagues envious).

150 g plain xylitol chocolate (50 g for melting + 100 g for chocolate chips)
50 g gluten-free plain white flour
15 g cocoa powder
55 g finely chopped walnuts
a pinch of salt
2 large eggs
180 g xylitol
1 tsp vanilla extract
100 g sugar-free mayonnaise

1. Pre-heat the oven to 160C/325F/gas mark 3. Line a 24 cm square cake tin with non-stick baking paper.

2. Put 50 g of chocolate in a heat-proof bowl and balance it over a saucepan which has some water in it. Heat gently to melt the chocolate. Stir occasionally. When the chocolate has melted, set aside.

3. Sift the flour and cocoa powder and put them into a bowl. Mix in the salt, walnuts and chocolate chips/chocolate cut into small pieces.

4. Whisk the xylitol and eggs together with an electric whisk until the volume triples.

5. Fold in the dry ingredients, melted chocolate, vanilla extract and mayonnaise.

6. Spoon the mixture into the baking tin, level with the back of a spoon and bake for 30-35 minutes or until a skewer inserted into the centre comes out clean.

7. Leave to cool in the tin. When cooled, cut into 16 squares.

* Substitutions

If you can't eat nuts, just leave the walnuts out.

Try something different

If you want to add a touch of milkiness into your brownies, use fructose-sweetened milk chocolate or xylitol-sweetened No Added Sugar Alternative to Milk Chocolate instead of plain xylitol chocolate (see pp. 40-41 for more details). Or you could use plain chocolate for melting and the 'milk' variety for the chocolate chips (this is my favourite combination).

Because the 'milk' chocolates are sweeter tasting than the plain chocolate, you may want to reduce the amount of xylitol to about 150-160 g.

Coffee makes it possible to get out of bed. Chocolate makes it worthwhile.

- Author unknown

Gluten-free
Wheat-free
Sugar-free
Yeast-free
Soya-free
Egg-free
Nut-free
Peanut-free
Vegetarian

* Dairy-free
* Casein-free
* Lactose-free
* Vegan

Pear crumble

Serves 4-5

This pear crumble recipe is a twist on the traditional apple crumble. The addition of ginger gives a lovely warmness to the pears and highlights their natural flavour.

Crumble topping
50 g unsalted butter
50 g gluten-free plain white flour
50 g fine polenta
50 g xylitol

Filling
8 small or 5 large pears
½ tsp ground ginger
1 tbsp corn flour

1. Pre-heat the oven to 180C/350F/gas mark 4.

2. To make the crumble topping, put the butter, flour and polenta into a bowl and rub them with your fingertips until they have combined and become crumbs. Add the xylitol and rub it into the crumbs. Set aside.

3. Peel, core and chop the pears into small pieces and place in an 18 cm round glass or

earthenware baking dish. Stir in the ground ginger and corn flour.

4. Spoon the crumble over the pears. Bake for 40-45 minutes, until the crumble looks golden yellow.

* Substitutions

You can make this crumble vegan, dairy-, lactose- and casein-free by substituting butter for non-dairy vegetable margarine.

Serving ideas

Serve hot, warm or cold; on its own or with Vanilla cream (p. 200), Custard (p. 202) or Custard ice cream (p. 204).

What to do with leftovers

You could use the leftovers to make pear crumble ice cream. Just follow the Custard ice cream recipe (p. 204) and mix in the left-over crumble after the custard has cooled to room temperature and before you put the container into a freezer.

Gluten-free
Wheat-free
Sugar-free
Yeast-free
Soya-free
Egg-free
Nut-free
Peanut-free
Corn-free
Vegetarian

* Lactose-free

Sticky rice pudding

Serves 2-3

This is a superb supper for those evenings when it's cold and dark outside and you crave comfort food.

110 g Thai sticky rice
310 ml water
a pinch of salt
1 tsp vanilla extract
150 ml single cream
2-3 tbsp Sweet Freedom
a sprinkle of ground cinnamon (optional)

1. Put the rice and water into a saucepan and bring to the boil. When the water starts boiling, put a lid on, turn the heat down and simmer for 12 minutes. Take off the heat, don't lift the lid, but leave the rice to stand for 5 minutes.

2. Stir in the salt, vanilla, cream and Sweet Freedom.

3. Divide into serving dishes and, if you like, sprinkle some cinnamon on top.

* Substitutions

To make the treat lactose-free, substitute single cream for Lactofree cream.

Serving ideas

Serve on its own or with tropical fruit, such as mangos and bananas.

Food for thought is no substitute for the real thing.

- Walt Kelly

Fruity favourites

Yellow fruit salad with passion fruit and vanilla sauce

Serves 4-6

I had a fruit salad similar to this at my favourite restaurant, Paul Ainsworth at Number 6 in Padstow, Cornwall – and I absolutely loved it. As soon as I got home, I had to try to replicate what Paul had prepared. This fruit salad is just gorgeous.

1 medium ripe pineapple
1 lemon, juice
2 eating apples
2 clementines
2 passion fruit
¼ tsp vanilla extract
2 tsp Sweet Freedom

1. Peel the pineapple and cut vertically into four segments. Cut off the hard cores. Then cut the pieces into very thin slices. Spread them around a flat serving plate.

2. Squeeze the lemon juice into a small bowl.

3. Peel and core the apples. Slice them thinly and dip into the lemon juice. (This will prevent them from discolouring.) Then spread the slices over the pineapple.

4. Peel the clementines. Cut them into thin slices or halve each segment lengthwise. Spread them on top of the other fruit.

5. Scoop the passion fruit flesh into a small bowl. Stir in the vanilla extract and Sweet Freedom, and spoon over the fruit.

Serving ideas

Serve as it is or with a dollop of clotted cream.

Gluten-free
Wheat-free
Sugar-free
Yeast-free
Soya-free
Dairy-free
Casein-free
Lactose-free
Egg-free
Nut-free
Peanut-free
Corn-free
Fat free
Vegetarian
Vegan

Strawberry and banana ice lollies

Makes 4-5

These ice lollies are loved by children: they will enjoy both eating and making them. Parents love them as well, especially since they're super healthy.

Make sure you use ripe bananas as they will make the ice lollies taste better.

3 medium bananas
250 g strawberries
1 tbsp Sweet Freedom

1. Thoroughly blitz all the ingredients in an electric chopper, blender or food processor.

2. Divide the purée into ice lolly moulds and freeze for at least 6 hours.

Serving ideas

For a more adult version, freeze the purée in freezable moulds, such as plastic containers. Once frozen, pop the treats out onto plates before serving. A dollop of Vanilla cream (p. 200) will complete the dish wonderfully.

Try something different

Combine other berries or fruit with the banana. For example, blueberries or mangos work particularly well.

Gluten-free
Wheat-free
Sugar-free
Yeast-free
Soya-free
Dairy-free
Casein-free
Lactose-free
Egg-free
Nut-free
Peanut-free
Corn-free
Fat-free
Vegetarian
Vegan

Poached pears

Serves 5

This recipe was inspired by a dessert that we made in a class at Ashburton Cookery School. In the original recipe the pears were poached in red wine, but my recipe uses the next best alternative – red grape juice – which makes the treat light.

5 small pears, for example Williams or Comice
1 litre red grape juice
1 cinnamon stick
3 cloves
1 lemon, juice and 2 slices of zest
1 orange, juice and 2 slices of zest
2 tbsp Sweet Freedom

1. Pour the red grape juice into a saucepan.

2. Add the cinnamon, cloves and Sweet Freedom.

3. Cut two thin slices of orange and lemon zest and add to the saucepan. Squeeze the juices from both fruits and add them as well.

4. Peel the pears, halve them and remove the seeds. If you want to serve the pears

'standing up' as opposed to on their sides, cut small pieces off from the bottom so that they will stand on their own. Place them in the saucepan.

5. Cut a circular piece of baking paper that covers the top of the saucepan and place it on the poaching liquid. This will help to keep the pears immersed. A cake tin liner will also work well.

6. Heat until the liquid starts boiling, then reduce the heat and gently poach the pears for 10 minutes.

7. Leave the pears in the poaching liquid until you're ready to serve.

Serving ideas

Serve hot or cold, with Vanilla cream (p. 200) or Custard ice cream (p. 204). You could also serve them with Cinnamon cream (p. 201) or Cinnamon ice cream (p. 206).

What to do
with leftovers

You can leave the pears in the poaching liquid for up to 48 hours if you keep them in a refrigerator. In fact, they will taste better the longer they remain in the liquid.

Any leftover pears are great for breakfast the following morning: serve with natural yogurt or gluten-free porridge, or use them instead of strawberries in Strawberry boost (p. 66).

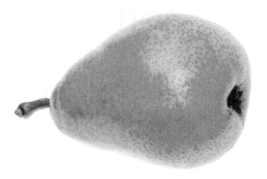

Stressed spelled backwards is
desserts. Coincidence? I think not.
- Author unknown

Gluten-free
Wheat-free
Sugar-free
Yeast-free
Soya-free
Dairy-free
Casein-free
Lactose-free
Egg-free
Nut-free
Peanut-free
Corn-free
Fat-free
Vegetarian
Vegan

Instant mango sorbet

Serves 2-3

This is a very quick and easy treat to make and it's ideal whenever unexpected guests arrive. Keep a ready supply of frozen mango pieces in your freezer and you can whizz a delightful treat within minutes.

You can buy frozen mango pieces in a super-market or chop fresh mangos into pieces and freeze them yourself.

250 g frozen mango pieces
80-120 ml apple juice
Sweet Freedom to taste

1. Put the frozen mango pieces and 80 ml of apple juice into an electric chopper or a food processor and blitz. Add more juice if needed.

2. Taste and add Sweet Freedom if the sorbet is not sweet enough (this will depend on how sweet your mangos are and how sweet you prefer your sorbet). Serve immediately.

Try something different

You can use other fruit and berries to make sorbet. For example, frozen strawberries, blueberries or a tropical fruit mix work wonderfully (you can buy all of these in a supermarket). If you are using berries, you won't need as much apple juice as the recipe states. If you are using a tropical fruit mix, the amount of apple juice is about the same.

Baked chocolate-centre bananas

Serves 6

Chocolate and banana are made to be eaten together, and when they're served hot, their gooey loveliness is just impossible to resist.

6 bananas
100 g plain xylitol chocolate

1. Pre-heat the oven to 180C/350F/gas mark 4.

2. Wash the bananas with their skins on and put them into a glass or earthenware oven-proof dish.

3. Make a long cut on the top side of each banana from one end to another, but don't make the cut so deep that it goes through to the other side. The aim is to make a 'pocket' for the chocolate.

4. If you're using a chocolate bar, snap it into squares first. Insert the chocolate pieces or drops into the cuts in the bananas.

5. Cover the dish with aluminium foil and bake for about 30 minutes.

Serving ideas

Serve the bananas straightaway on their own or with Vanilla cream (p. 200) or Custard ice cream (p. 204).

Try something different

If you'd rather use a milkier chocolate variety, try fructose-sweetened chocolate or xylitol-sweetened No Added Sugar Alternative to Milk Chocolate (see pp. 40-41 for more details).

Baked bananas make an excellent dessert at a barbeque. Wrap each banana individually inside some aluminium foil and cook on the grill.

Gluten-free
Wheat-free
Sugar-free
Yeast-free
Soya-free
Egg-free
Nut-free
Peanut-free
Corn-free
Vegetarian

* Dairy-free
* Casein-free
* Lactose-free
* Vegan

Baked peaches with raspberry sauce
Serves 4

Baked peaches make a fantastic light dessert after any meal and they're also thoroughly enjoyable on their own as an afternoon treat or supper. Their juicy sweetness combined with the sharpness of raspberries is simply delectable.

It's best to use ripe peaches. So if you buy them in August or September when they're in season, you're more likely to find really juicy ones.

4 ripe peaches
2-3 tbsp Sweet Freedom
1 tsp vanilla extract
1 tbsp unsalted butter
170 g raspberries

1. Pre-heat the oven to 200C/400F/gas mark 6.

2. Halve the peaches and remove the stones. Place them cut side up on an oven-proof dish.

3. Mix the vanilla extract and 2 tbsp of Sweet Freedom in a small bowl or cup.

4. Brush the peaches with the mixture. You should have some mixture left over. Set this aside.

5. Place a tiny piece of butter on each peach half.

6. Bake the peaches for 15-20 minutes until they are tender and caramelised.

7. While the peaches are in the oven, make the raspberry sauce. Put the raspberries in a sieve and press them through with the back of a spoon so that the seeds remain in the sieve and the liquid goes through into a bowl underneath.

8. Add the remaining Sweet Freedom and vanilla mixture into the raspberry sauce. Taste and add more Sweet Freedom if the sauce is not sweet enough.

9. Serve hot or cold with some raspberry sauce spooned over the peaches.

Chocolate's okay, but I prefer a
really intense fruit taste. You know
when a peach is absolutely perfect...
it's sublime. I'd like to capture that
and then use it in a dessert.
- Kathy Mattea

* Substitutions

To make the treat vegan, dairy-, lactose- and casein-free, use non-dairy vegetable margarine instead of butter.

Serving ideas

If you're serving the peaches hot, Custard ice cream (p. 204) makes a lovely accompaniment.

Baked apples

Serves 4

Baked apples are so easy to make and so comforting to eat. They make a great pudding or supper.

4 large eating apples

Filling
2 heaped tsp raisins
2 dried figs
2 dried dates
1 tsp ground cinnamon
½ orange, juice and zest
1-2 tsp Sweet Freedom (optional)

1. Start by making the filling. Zest and juice half an orange and put in a small bowl. Chop the figs and dates into tiny pieces and add them together with the raisins and cinnamon into the bowl. If you prefer your baked apples sweeter, also add Sweet Freedom. Mix and leave to stand for about 15 minutes or until the dried fruit have absorbed the orange juice.

2. While the dried fruit are standing, pre-heat the oven to 180C/350F/gas mark 4.

3. Core the apples and place them on a glass or earthenware oven dish.

4. Fill the cored holes with the dried fruit.

5. Bake in the oven for about 40 minutes or until juices start to come out of the apples and they are soft inside.

Serving ideas

Serve hot or cold, on their own or with Vanilla cream (p. 200), Cinnamon cream (p. 201), Custard (p. 202), Custard ice cream (p. 204) or Cinnamon ice cream (p. 206).

Try something different

Try different kinds of fillings and experiment with other dried fruit. For example, dried apricots or dried cranberries go well with raisins and sultanas.

The kitchen is a country in which there are always discoveries to be made.

- Grimond de la Reynière

Delightful drinks

Gluten-free
Wheat-free
Sugar-free
Yeast-free
Soya-free
Egg-free
Nut-free
Peanut-free
Corn-free
Vegetarian

* Dairy-free
* Casein-free
* Lactose-free
* Vegan

Hot chocolate

Serves 4

This is a rich and velvety drink, ideal for those dark and cold winter nights when you just want to snuggle on the sofa and read a good book or watch your favourite TV programme.

1 litre milk
75 g plain xylitol chocolate
2 tsp vanilla extract
1-6 tbsp xylitol or Sweet Freedom

1. Put the milk, chocolate, vanilla extract and 1 tbsp of sweetener in a saucepan and gently bring to the boil. Stir constantly.

2. Take off the heat and taste. Add more sweetener if needed.

* Substitutions

To make the drink lactose-free, use Lactofree milk (please note that lactose-free milk burns easily, so be extra careful). To make the drink vegan, dairy- and casein-free, use rice or soya drink.

Gluten-free
Wheat-free
Sugar-free
Yeast-free
Soya-free
Egg-free
Nut-free
Peanut-free
Corn-free
Vegetarian

* Low lactose

Mango lassi

Serves 2

Lassi is a yogurt-based drink from South Asia. Kesar mangos make the best lassi as they are incredibly sweet and juicy. If you can't get hold of them, use any large ripe mango.

200 g natural yogurt
125 ml milk
1 large ripe mango or 2-3 Kesar mangos
Sweet Freedom to taste
¼ tsp ground cardamom (optional)

1. Put the yogurt, milk and chopped mango pieces into a blender or food processor and blitz for a couple of minutes.

2. Taste and add Sweet Freedom if need be. Pour into glasses and sprinkle some cardamom on top. Serve chilled.

* Substitutions

To make the lassi low in lactose, use Lactofree milk and natural yogurt with probiotics (bio-cultures) or goat's milk yogurt.

Still lemonade

Serves 2-3

This is a summery drink that's great for barbecues and picnics.

2 lemons, juice
500 ml cold water
3-5 tbsp xylitol
ice cubes (optional)
lemon slices (optional)

1. Squeeze the lemon juice into a jug. Add water and 3 tbsp of xylitol. Stir until the xylitol dissolves. Taste the lemonade and add more xylitol if needed.

2. Keep refrigerated until you're ready to serve the drink. Best served with ice cubes and slices of lemons.

Try something different

Freeze strawberries or grapes (or buy frozen strawberries) and use them instead of ice cubes.

Gluten-free
Wheat-free
Sugar-free
Yeast-free
Soya-free
Dairy-free
Casein-free
Lactose-free
Egg-free
Nut-free
Peanut-free
Corn-free
Fat-free
Vegetarian
Vegan

Ginger ale

Serves 3-5

This ginger ale has a real kick to it. It's refreshing, yet warming at the same time.

150 g ginger root
200 ml still water
170 g Sweet Freedom
2 limes, juice
750 ml sparkling water
ice cubes

1. Slice the ginger thinly and put it into a saucepan together with still water and Sweet Freedom. Bring to the boil, reduce the heat and gently simmer for 20 minutes. Then let the syrupy liquid cool to room temperature.

2. Squeeze the juice of the limes into a serving jug. Add the liquid from the saucepan through a sieve. Pour in the sparkling water and mix.

3. Put in a refrigerator until you're ready to serve. Add ice cubes before serving.

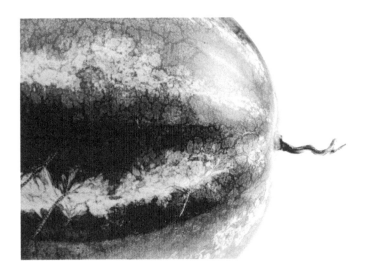

When one has tasted watermelon he knows what the angels eat.

- Mark Twain

Gluten-free
Wheat-free
Sugar-free
Yeast-free
Soya-free
Dairy-free
Casein-free
Lactose-free
Egg-free
Nut-free
Peanut-free
Corn-free
Fat-free
Vegetarian
Vegan

Watermelon and strawberry drink

Serves 2

This is a thick drink, bordering on a smoothie. It's not too sweet which makes it thirst quenching on a hot summer's day.

500 g (about ½) watermelon
200 g strawberries
1 lime, juice
ice cubes

1. De-seed the watermelon and cut it into chunks.

2. Squeeze the juice of the lime.

3. Put the watermelon, strawberries and lime juice into an electric chopper, blender or food processor and blitz thoroughly.

4. Pour the juice into a small jug or glasses and refrigerate until you're ready to serve it. Add ice cubes just before serving.

Gluten-free
Wheat-free
Sugar-free
Yeast-free
Soya-free
Dairy-free
Casein-free
Lactose-free
Egg-free
Nut-free
Peanut-free
Corn-free
Fat-free
Vegetarian
Vegan

Fruity ice tea

Serves 5-6

This is a cooling summer drink. Make a jugful in the morning and you'll have a delicious drink to keep you going for the rest of the day.

1 litre boiling water
5 Darjeeling teabags
3-5 tbsp xylitol
200 g strawberries
2 oranges
ice cubes

1. Put the teabags into a jug and pour boiling water over them. Let them stay immersed for 2-3 minutes before taking them out.

2. Mix in the xylitol and let the tea cool.

3. Squeeze the juice of 1 ½ oranges and mix in with the tea.

4. Slice the remaining orange half and the strawberries and add to the tea.

5. Keep the jug in a refrigerator until you're ready to serve. Just before serving, add ice cubes.

Gluten-free
Wheat-free
Sugar-free
Yeast-free
Soya-free
Egg-free
Nut-free
Peanut-free
Corn-free
Vegetarian

* Low lactose

Vanilla smoothie

Serves 4

This drink is a perfect snack when you don't have much time but would like something delicious.

600 g natural yogurt
200 ml apple juice
80 g Sweet Freedom
1 tbsp vanilla extract

1. Whisk all the ingredients together in a jug.

2. Keep in a refrigerator until you're ready to serve.

* Substitutions

To make a low-lactose smoothie, use natural yogurt with probiotics (bio-cultures) or goat's milk yogurt with probiotics.

Too much of a good thing can be wonderful.

- Mae West

Alluring accompaniments

Vanilla cream

Gluten-free
Wheat-free
Sugar-free
Yeast-free
Soya-free
Egg-free
Nut-free
Peanut-free
Corn-free
Vegetarian

* Lactose-free

Vanilla cream is very versatile and can be used to accompany many desserts. You can also serve it on its own with fresh fruit.

Small portion
150 ml whipping cream
¾ tsp vanilla extract
15-20 g xylitol

Large portion
300 ml whipping cream
1 ½ tsp vanilla extract
30-40 g xylitol

1. Place all the ingredients in a bowl and whisk until soft peaks form.

2. Keep refrigerated until you're ready to serve.

* Substitutions

If you want lactose-free vanilla cream, use Lactofree cream.

Gluten-free
Wheat-free
Sugar-free
Yeast-free
Soya-free
Egg-free
Nut-free
Peanut-free
Corn-free
Vegetarian

* Lactose-free

Cinnamon cream

Cinnamon cream is a fantastic accompaniment to puddings and cakes that have, for example, apple in them.

Small portion
150 ml whipping cream
¾ tsp vanilla extract
15-20 g xylitol
¼ tsp ground cinnamon

Large portion
300 ml whipping cream
1 ½ tsp vanilla extract
30-40 g xylitol
½ tsp ground cinnamon

1. Place all the ingredients in a bowl and whisk until soft peaks form.

2. Keep refrigerated until you're ready to serve.

* Substitutions

For a lactose-free option, use Lactofree cream.

Gluten-free
Wheat-free
Sugar-free
Yeast-free
Soya-free
Nut-free
Peanut-free
Vegetarian

* Lactose-free

Custard

I love custard. I could eat it on its own, hot or cold, for breakfast, lunch and dinner.

You can determine the thickness of your custard by how much corn flour you use: 2 tsp will be fairly runny when hot but it will thicken as it cools. Use more corn flour when you want your custard thicker.

600 ml single cream
5 large egg yolks
2 tsp vanilla extract
2-5 tsp corn flour
75 g xylitol

1. Put all the ingredients apart from the cream into a large wide-necked jug and mix thoroughly.

2. Put the cream into a saucepan and bring to the boil on a gentle heat, stirring constantly.

3. Take the cream off the heat and pour it slowly into the jug whilst whisking all the time.

4. Pour the mixture back into the saucepan (or if you detect any signs of burning on the bot-

tom or edges of the saucepan, transfer to a fresh saucepan) and gently heat without boiling until the custard has thickened. This should take 1-2 minutes. If the custard starts to separate and becomes granular, this means that it has over-heated. You can get it back to a smooth consistency by taking the saucepan off the heat and cooling the custard by whisking it until it becomes smooth again.

* Substitutions

You can make this custard lactose-free by substituting ordinary cream for Lactofree cream.

Serving ideas

Serve hot or cold, on its own or with fresh fruit, or make it an accompaniment to other treats, such as Apple cake (p. 138), Pear crumble (p. 164) or Lemon loaf (p. 158).

Gluten-free
Wheat-free
Sugar-free
Yeast-free
Soya-free
Nut-free
Peanut-free
Corn-free
Vegetarian

* Lactose-free

Custard ice cream

Serves 4-6 on its own or 8-10 as an accompaniment to another treat

Like custard, custard ice cream is just irresistible. It's good to have a portion in the freezer at all times, in case of any unexpected guests (or if you just happen to fancy something nice at a moment's notice...)

The consistency of this ice cream is quite hard, so let it thaw a little before serving.

600 ml double cream
75 g xylitol
2 tsp vanilla extract
4 large egg yolks

1. Separate the egg whites from the yolks and put the yolks into a large wide-necked jug.

2. Place the cream, xylitol and vanilla extract in a saucepan and bring to the boil over a gentle heat. Stir constantly with a whisk.

3. When the mixture starts to boil, take it off the heat and pour slowly into the jug whilst whisking the mixture all the time.

4. Pour into a container that is suitable for freezing and leave to cool at room temperature. Once cooled, place the container in a freezer. Leave to freeze overnight.

* Substitutions

To make your ice cream lactose-free, use Lactofree cream. However, because the fat content of the Lactofree cream is lower than that of double cream, it's more prone to developing ice crystals. Therefore, you should stir the ice cream every 1-2 hours during the freezing process.

Serving ideas

Serve on its own or with fresh fruit, or make it an accompaniment to treats that are served hot, such as Apple cake (p. 138), Torte de banana (p. 110), Poached pears (p. 174) or Pear crumble (p. 164).

Gluten-free
Wheat-free
Sugar-free
Yeast-free
Soya-free
Nut-free
Peanut-free
Corn-free
Vegetarian

* Lactose-free

Cinnamon ice cream

Serves 4-6 on its own or 8-10 as an accompaniment to another treat

This cinnamon ice cream is lovely and not too overpowering. As with Custard ice cream, its consistency is quite hard, so you'll need to let it soften at room temperature before serving.

600 ml double cream
75 g xylitol
2 tsp vanilla extract
¾ tsp ground cinnamon
4 large egg yolks

1. Separate the egg whites from the yolks and put the yolks in a large wide-necked jug.

2. Place the cream, xylitol, cinnamon and vanilla extract in a saucepan and bring to the boil over a gentle heat. Stir constantly with a whisk.

3. When the mixture starts to boil, take off the heat and pour slowly into the jug whilst whisking the mixture all the time.

4. Pour into a container that is suitable for freezing and leave to cool at room temperature. Once cooled, place the container in a freezer. Leave to freeze overnight.

* Substitutions

You can make lactose-free Cinnamon ice cream by using Lactofree cream. However, because the fat content of the Lactofree cream is lower than that of double cream, it's more prone to developing ice crystals. Therefore, you should stir the ice cream every 1-2 hours during the freezing process.

Serving ideas

Serve on its own or with fresh fruit or stewed apple. You can also make it an accompaniment to hot puddings that might benefit from additional cinnamon flavour, such as Apple cake (p. 138) or Poached pears (p. 174).

Eating is not merely a material pleasure. Eating well gives a spectacular joy to life and contributes immensely to goodwill and happy companionship. It is of great importance to the morale.

- Elsa Schiaparelli

Conversion tables

Weight				Dimension	
Metric (grams)	**Imperial (pounds/ ounces)**			**Metric (centimetres)**	**Imperial (inches)**
10 g	½ oz			1 cm	½ inch
20 g	¾ oz			2 cm	¾ inch
25 g	1 oz			3 cm	1 ¼ inches
40 g	1 ½ oz			4 cm	1 ½ inches
50 g	2 oz			5 cm	2 inches
60 g	2 ½ oz			6 cm	2 ½ inches
75 g	3 oz			7.5 cm	3 inches
100 g	3 ½ oz			9 cm	3 ½ inches
110 g	4 oz			10 cm	4 inches
125 g	4 ½ oz			13 cm	5 inches
150 g	5 oz			15 cm	6 inches
175 g	6 oz			16 cm	6 ½ inches
200 g	7 oz			18 cm	7 inches
225 g	8 oz			19 cm	7 ½ inches
250 g	9 oz			20 cm	8 inches
275 g	10 oz			23 cm	9 inches
300 g	10 ½ oz			24 cm	9 ½ inches
325 g	11 oz			25.5 cm	10 inches
350 g	12 oz			28 cm	11 inches
375 g	13 oz			30 cm	12 inches
400 g	14 oz				
425 g	15 oz				
450 g	1 lb				
500 g	1 lb 2 oz				
700 g	1 ½ lb				
900 g	2 lb				
1000 g = 1 kg	2 lb 3 oz				

Please note that the conversions are approximations and have been rounded either up or down.

Volume

Metric (millilitres/ litres)	Imperial (fluid ounces)	Imperial (pints)	Teaspoons and tablespoons
1.25 ml			¼ tsp
2.5 ml			½ tsp
5 ml			1 tsp
15 ml	½ fl oz		1 tbsp = 3 tsp
25 ml	1 fl oz		
55 ml	2 fl oz		
75 ml	3 fl oz		
100 ml	3 ½ fl oz		
150 ml	5 fl oz	¼ pt	
275 ml	10 fl oz	½ pt	
425 ml	15 fl oz	¾ pt	
570 ml	20 fl oz	1 pt	
725 ml		1 ¼ pt	
1000 ml = 1 l		1 ¾ pt	
1.2 l		2 pt	

Volume - American measures

Metric (millilitres)	American (cups/pints)
30 ml	⅛ cup
60 ml	¼ cup
120 ml	½ cup
180 ml	¾ cup
240 ml	1 cup
480 ml	1 pint

Please note that the American pint is different from the imperial pint used in Britain.

Research tells us fourteen out of any ten individuals like chocolate.

- Sandra Boynton

Resources

Ingredients, products and manufacturers

Arla Foods' Lactofree range
www.lactofree.co.uk
www.arla.com
Lactose-free dairy products

Clearspring
www.clearspring.co.uk
Organic Japanese and European foods, including agar flakes
and no-added-sugar fruit purées and fruit spreads

Delamere Dairy
www.delameredairy.co.uk
Goat's milk, butter, cheese, yogurts and soya drinks

Doves Farm
www.dovesfarm.co.uk
Organic and gluten-free flour specialists who also sell gluten-
free biscuits, breakfast cereals and pasta

Hotel Chocolat
www.hotelchocolat.co.uk
100% pure dark chocolate

Meridian Foods
www.meridianfoods.co.uk
Organic and natural foods, including gluten- and dairy-free
sauces, nut spreads and fruit spreads with no added sugar

Plamil
www.plamilfoods.co.uk
Vegan, gluten-, wheat-, dairy- and nut-free foods, including
no-added-sugar chocolate (made with xylitol) and egg- and
sugar-free mayonnaise

Provamel
www.provamel.co.uk
Non-dairy alternatives to various dairy products

Rice Dream
www.ricedream.co.uk
Non-dairy alternative to milk

St. Dalfour
www.stdalfour.co.uk
Fruit spreads with no added sugar

Sweet Freedom
www.sweetfreedom.co.uk
Sweetening syrup made from fruit (apples, grapes, carob)

Total Sweet
www.totalsweet.co.uk
Xylitol sweetener/granules

Willie's Cacao
www.williescacao.com
Pure 100% cacao bars

Woodlands Dairy
www.woodlandsdairy.co.uk
Goat's milk yogurt

Xylitol UK
www.xylitolshop.co.uk
Xylitol products, including the sweetener itself as well as xylitol honey, chocolates, jam and ketchup

Xylo Brit
www.xylobrit.co.uk
Xylitol sweetener/granules

Xylo Sweet
www.xlear.com/xylosweet.aspx
An American website selling xylitol

Shopping sites

Health food shops

Dietary Needs Direct
www.dietaryneedsdirect.co.uk
An online shop selling products suitable for special diets and
natural healthcare

Evergreen Health Food Stores
www.evergreenhealthstore.co.uk
An online health food shop

GoodnessDirect
www.goodnessdirect.co.uk
An online health food shop

Greenlife
www.greenlife.co.uk
A health food store based in Totnes, Devon; also has an online
shop

Holland & Barrett
www.hollandandbarrett.com
A retailer of natural food supplements and health foods that
also has an online shop

The Natural Grocery Store
www.naturalgrocery.co.uk
An organic online grocery store

Planet Organic
www.planetorganic.com
A health food store with branches in London; also has an
online shop

Supermarkets online

Sainsbury's
www.sainsburys.co.uk

Tesco
www.tesco.co.uk

Waitrose
www.waitrose.co.uk

Other shopping sites

Merton Books
http://mertonbooksonline.co.uk
An online shop for books on allergies and restricted diets

Medical conditions and special diets

ADHD

AADD-UK – Adult Attention Deficit Disorder UK
http://aadduk.org
A UK charity providing information on and raising awareness of ADHD in adulthood

ADDISS – The National Attention Deficit Disorder Information and Support Service
www.addiss.co.uk
A UK charity providing information and resources on ADHD

Hyperactive Children's Support Group
www.hacsg.org.uk
A UK charity helping hyperactive children and their families

Mind
www.mind.org.uk
A UK charity providing information and advice on mental health issues, including ADHD, and campaigning to promote and protect good mental health

Misunderstood
www.misunderstood.org.uk
A UK charity supporting people with ADHD and their families

NHS Choices – ADHD
www.nhs.uk/Conditions/Attention-deficit-hyperactivity-disorder
Information on ADHD

Allergy, intolerance and sensitivity

Action against Allergy (AAA)
www.actionagainstallergy.co.uk
A UK charity providing information on allergies

Allergy UK
www.allergyuk.org
A medical charity for people with allergy, food intolerance and chemical sensitivity

Anaphylaxis Campaign
www.anaphylaxis.org.uk
A UK charity providing information and support to people with severe allergic reactions to foods and other triggers (for example, latex, drugs, insect stings)

Blossom Campaign
www.blossomcampaign.org
A children's campaign organised by Allergy UK providing information on and promoting the awareness of childhood allergies

British Society for Allergy and Clinical Immunology
www.bsaci.org
A national, professional and academic society aiming to improve the management of allergies and related diseases of immune system through education, training and research

Corn Allergens
www.cornallergens.com
A US website containing information on corn allergy

Food Intolerance Awareness
www.foodintoleranceawareness.org
A division of Allergy UK providing information on food intolerance

Food Reactions
www.foodreactions.org
Information on disorders and conditions caused by ingestion of certain foods

Food Standards Agency
http://food.gov.uk
An independent government department set up to protect the public's health and consumer interests in relation to food; the Safety and Hygiene section has information on food allergies

Foundation for Allergy Information and Research (FAIR)
www.allergyresearch.info
A research organisation focussing on allergies

NHS Choices – Food Allergy
www.nhs.uk/conditions/food-allergy
Information on food allergies

NHS Choices – Lactose Intolerance
www.nhs.uk/conditions/lactose-intolerance
Information on lactose intolerance

Peanut Allergy UK
http://peanutallergyuk.co.uk
A non-profit organisation supporting people with peanut allergy

Autism spectrum disorders

Ambitious about Autism
www.ambitiousaboutautism.org.uk
A UK charity for children and young people with autism

Autism Independent UK
www.autismuk.com
An organisation working to improve the quality of life for people living with autism and raising awareness of the condition

National Autistic Society
www.autism.org.uk
A UK charity providing information and support for people with autism, including Asperger syndrome

NHS Choices – Autistic Spectrum Disorder
www.nhs.uk/conditions/Autistic-spectrum-disorder
Information on autistic spectrum disorders

Research Autism
www.researchautism.net
A UK charity dedicated to research into interventions in autism

Coeliac disease

coeliacsmatter.com
www.coeliacsmatter.com
Information on coeliac disease and gluten-free diet

Coeliac UK
www.coeliac.org.uk
A charity campaigning and giving information and support for people with coeliac disease and dermatitis herpetiformis

NHS Choices – Coeliac Disease
www.nhs.uk/conditions/coeliac-disease
Information on coeliac disease

Diabetes and hypoglycaemia

Diabetes.co.uk
www.diabetes.co.uk
A website and online community providing support and information on diabetes

Diabetes Research and Wellness Foundation
www.drwf.org.uk
A UK charity working towards discovering the cure for diabetes as well as supporting, advising and educating people living with the condition

Diabetes UK
www.diabetes.org.uk
A UK charity providing information, funding research, campaigning and helping people with diabetes

Insulin Dependent Diabetes Trust
www.iddtinternational.org
A UK charity providing information and support for people with diabetes and raising awareness of related issues

Juvenile Diabetic Research Foundation
www.jdrf.org.uk
A UK charity funding type 1 diabetes research

NHS Choices – Diabetes
www.nhs.uk/conditions/Diabetes
Information on diabetes

NHS Choices – Hyperglycaemia
www.nhs.uk/conditions/Hyperglycaemia
Information on hyperglycaemia and diabetes

Fibromyalgia

FibroAction
www.fibroaction.org
A UK charity raising awareness of fibromyalgia

Fibromyalgia Association Scotland
www.fmascotland.org.uk
A Scottish charity providing information, advice and support for people with fibromyalgia

Fibromyalgia Association UK
www.fibromyalgia-associationuk.org
A registered UK charity providing information, raising awareness and supporting people with fibromyalgia and their families

National Fibromyalgia and Chronic Pain Association
www.fmcpaware.org
A US non-profit organisation providing support and information to people with chronic pain illnesses

National Fibromyalgia Association
www.fmaware.org
A US non-profit organisation providing information, raising awareness and offering support to people affected by fibromyalgia

NHS Choices – Fibromyalgia
www.nhs.uk/conditions/Fibromyalgia
Information on fibromyalgia

UK Fibromyalgia
www.ukfibromyalgia.com
Information on fibromyalgia

Irritable bowel syndrome (IBS)

IBS Research Update
www.ibsresearchupdate.org
A website of a charitable research programme run by medical professionals treating IBS patients

IBS Self Help and Support Group
www.ibsgroup.org
A US organisation providing information and support for people with IBS

NHS Choices – Irritable Bowel Syndrome
www.nhs.uk/conditions/Irritable-bowel-syndrome
Information on IBS

ME and chronic fatigue syndrome(CFS)

Association of Young People with ME
www.ayme.org.uk
A UK charity providing information and support to children and young people with ME

CFIDS Association of America
www.cfids.org
A US charitable organisation offering information on and raising awareness of chronic fatigue and immune dysfunction syndrome

Invest in ME
www.investinme.org
A UK charity campaigning for bio-medical research into ME

ME Association
www.meassociation.org.uk
A UK charity providing information, support and practical
advice for people affected with ME/CFS/Post Viral Fatigue
Syndrome

M.E. Support
www.mesupport.co.uk
An online community providing information on and raising
awareness of chronic fatigue illnesses

National M.E. Centre
www.nmec.org.uk
A centre based in Essex that offers care and support to
people affected by ME and their families

NHS Choices – Chronic Fatigue Syndrome
www.nhs.uk/conditions/Chronic-fatigue-syndrome
Information on CFS and ME

Veganism and vegetarianism

Vegan Society
www.vegansociety.com
An educational charity providing information and guidance
on various aspects of veganism

Vegetarian and Vegan Foundation
www.vegetarian.org.uk
A registered charity monitoring and explaining the scientific
research relating to the link between health and diet

Vegetarian Society
www.vegsoc.org
An educational charity supporting, representing and
increasing the number of vegetarians in the UK

Miscellaneous

Action on Pain
www.action-on-pain.co.uk
A UK charity providing support and advice to people affected by chronic pain

British Nutrition Foundation
www.nutrition.org.uk
A UK organisation providing evidence-based information on food and nutrition in the context of health and lifestyle

British Pain Society
www.britishpainsociety.org
An alliance of professionals advancing the understanding and management of pain for the benefit of people affected by pain

Contact a Family
www.cafamily.org.uk
A UK charity offering advice and support to families with disabled children and information on allergies, diabetes, coeliac disease, autism spectrum disorders, IBS, ME and CFS

Core
www.corecharity.org.uk
A UK charity funding research into the entire range of gut, liver, intestinal and bowel illnesses

Direct Gov: Healthy Living
www.direct.gov.uk/en/HealthAndWellBeing/HealthyLiving
The UK government's digital service website containing information on healthy living and links to further resources

foodsmatter.com
www.foodsmatter.com
A website with articles and reports on allergy, intolerance, sensitivities, coeliac disease, IBS, fibromyalgia, CFS, ME, candida and other health problems

FreeFrom Foods Matter
www.freefromfoodsmatter.com
An information website on 'free-from' foods

NHS Direct
www.nhsdirect.nhs.uk
National Health Service healthline, including health advice and information

Nutritionist Resource
www.nutritionist-resource.org.uk
Information on nutrition and help with finding a professional nutritionist near you

Pain Concern
www.painconcern.org.uk
A UK charity providing information for people living with pain

RADAR – The Royal Association for Disability Rights
http://radar-shop.org.uk
Information on the RADAR National Key Scheme (NKS) which provides keys for registered disabled people to access locked public toilets around the UK

Don't wreck a sublime chocolate experience by feeling guilty.

- Lora Brody

Recipe index

Recipe	Free from	Page
Apple and custard tart	Gluten, wheat, sugar, yeast, soya, nuts, peanuts + low-lactose option	112
Apple and mango jelly	Gluten, wheat, sugar, yeast, soya, dairy, casein, lactose, egg, nut, peanut, corn, fat	156
Apple cake	Gluten, wheat, sugar, yeast, soya, dairy, casein, lactose, peanut, corn	138
Apricot and oat flat bread	Gluten, wheat, sugar, yeast, soya, egg, nut, peanut, corn + dairy-, casein- and lactose-free option	80
Baked apples	Gluten, wheat, sugar, yeast, soya, dairy, casein, lactose, egg, nut, peanut, corn, fat	186
Baked chocolate-centre bananas	Gluten, wheat, sugar, yeast, soya, dairy, casein, lactose, egg, nut, peanut, corn	180
Baked peaches with raspberry sauce	Gluten, wheat, sugar, yeast, soya, egg, nut, peanut, corn + dairy-, casein- and lactose-free option	182
Banana bread	Gluten, wheat, sugar, yeast, soya, nut, peanut + low-lactose option	98
Biscotti	Gluten, wheat, sugar, yeast, soya, dairy, casein, lactose, peanut + nut-free option	88
Chocolate almond bites	Gluten, wheat, sugar, yeast, soya, peanut, corn + lactose-free option	96
Chocolate and vanilla celebration cake	Gluten, wheat, sugar, yeast, soya, nut, peanut + lactose-free option	122
Chocolate brownies	Gluten, wheat, sugar, yeast, soya, dairy, casein, lactose, peanut + nut-free option	160
Cinnamon cream	Gluten, wheat, sugar, yeast, soya, egg, nut, peanut, corn + lactose-free option	201

Recipe	Free from	Page
Cinnamon ice cream	Gluten, wheat, sugar, yeast, soya, nut, peanut, corn + lactose-free option	206
Coconut and chocolate truffles	Gluten, wheat, sugar, yeast, soya, egg, nut, peanut, corn	154
Coffee and pecan cake	Gluten, wheat, sugar, yeast, soya, peanut, corn + lactose-free option	116
Coffee granita	Gluten, wheat, sugar, yeast, soya, egg, nut, peanut, corn + lactose-free option	78
Creamy strawberry and passion fruit quark	Gluten, wheat, sugar, yeast, soya, egg, nut, peanut, corn + low-lactose and lactose-free options	76
Custard	Gluten, wheat, sugar, yeast, soya, nut, peanut + lactose-free option	202
Custard ice cream	Gluten, wheat, sugar, yeast, soya, nut, peanut, corn + lactose-free option	204
Date and walnut cake	Gluten, wheat, sugar, yeast, soya, peanut + dairy-, casein- and lactose-free option	90
Drop scones	Gluten, wheat, sugar, yeast, soya, nut, peanut + dairy-, casein- and lactose-free option	70
Fruit, nut and chocolate platter	Gluten, wheat, sugar, yeast, soya, egg, peanut, corn + lactose-free option	120
Fruity ice tea	Gluten, wheat, sugar, yeast, soya, dairy, casein, lactose, egg, nut, peanut, corn, fat	196
Ginger ale	Gluten, wheat, sugar, yeast, soya, dairy, casein, lactose, egg, nut, peanut, corn, fat	193
Grilled pineapple with pistachio ice cream	Gluten, wheat, sugar, yeast, soya, peanut, corn + lactose-free option	134
Heavenly chocolate cake	Gluten, wheat, sugar, yeast, soya, peanut, corn + lactose-free option	106

Recipe	Free from	Page
Hot chocolate	Gluten, wheat, sugar, yeast, soya, egg, nut, peanut, corn + dairy-, casein- and lactose-free option	190
Instant mango sorbet	Gluten, wheat, sugar, yeast, soya, dairy, casein, lactose, egg, nut, peanut, corn, fat	178
Lemon cheesecake	Gluten, wheat, sugar, yeast, soya, egg, nut, peanut + lactose-free option	102
Lemon delicious	Gluten, wheat, sugar, yeast, soya, dairy, casein, lactose, nut, peanut	142
Lemon loaf	Gluten, wheat, sugar, yeast, soya, peanut + dairy-, casein- and lactose-free option	158
Mango fool	Gluten, wheat, sugar, yeast, soya, egg, nut, peanut, corn + low-lactose option	140
Mango lassi	Gluten, wheat, sugar, yeast, soya, egg, nut, peanut, corn + low-lactose option	191
Milk chocolate mousse	Gluten, wheat, sugar, yeast, soya, nut, peanut, corn + lactose-free option	128
Mini mince tarts	Gluten, wheat, sugar, yeast, soya, egg, nut, peanut, corn + dairy-, casein- and lactose-free option	92
Nut and cranberry bars	Gluten, wheat, sugar, yeast, soya, dairy, casein, lactose, egg, peanut, corn	68
Orange and cranberry mini muffins	Gluten, wheat, sugar, yeast, soya, nut, peanut + dairy, casein- and lactose-free option	86
Pancakes	Gluten, wheat, sugar, yeast, soya, nut, peanut + dairy-, casein- and lactose-free option	152
Pear crumble	Gluten, wheat, sugar, yeast, soya, egg, nut, peanut + dairy-, casein- and lactose-free option	164
Poached pears	Gluten, wheat, sugar, yeast, soya, dairy, casein, lactose, egg, nut, peanut, corn, fat	174

Recipe	Free from	Page
Profiteroles	Gluten, wheat, sugar, yeast, soya, nut, peanut + lactose-free option	130
Pumpkin and rhubarb muffins	Gluten, wheat, sugar, yeast, soya, peanut + dairy-, casein- and lactose-free option	72
Sticky rice pudding	Gluten, wheat, sugar, yeast, soya, egg, nut, peanut, corn + lactose-free option	166
Still lemonade	Gluten, wheat, sugar, yeast, soya, dairy, casein, lactose, egg, nut, peanut, corn, fat	192
Strawberry and banana ice lollies	Gluten, wheat, sugar, yeast, soya, dairy, casein, lactose, egg, nut, peanut, corn, fat	172
Strawberry boost	Gluten, wheat, sugar, yeast, soya, egg, peanut, corn + nut-free and low-lactose options	66
Summer berry squares	Gluten, wheat, sugar, yeast, soya, peanut + dairy-, casein- and lactose-free option	84
Tiramisu	Gluten, wheat, sugar, yeast, soya, nut, peanut + lactose-free option	146
Torta de banana	Gluten, wheat, sugar, yeast, soya, nut, peanut + dairy-, casein- and lactose-free option	110
Vanilla cream	Gluten, wheat, sugar, yeast, soya, egg, nut, peanut, corn + lactose-free option	200
Vanilla smoothie	Gluten, wheat, sugar, yeast, soya, egg, nut, peanut, corn + low-lactose option	197
Watermelon and strawberry drink	Gluten, wheat, sugar, yeast, soya, dairy, casein, lactose, egg, nut, peanut, corn, fat	195
Yellow fruit salad with passion fruit and vanilla sauce	Gluten, wheat, sugar, yeast, soya, dairy, casein, lactose, egg, nut, peanut, corn, fat	170

Photo credits

Cover photograph © Liv Friis-larsen | Dreamstime.com

p. 14 © Sarit Saliman | Dreamstime.com

p. 19 © Olga Lupol | Dreamstime.com

p. 27 © Vclements | Dreamstime.com

p. 44 © Matthew Collingwood | Dreamstime.com

p. 48 © Tomasz Szadkowski | Dreamstime.com

p. 55 © Nilsz | Dreamstime.com

p. 62 © Agg | Dreamstime.com

p. 64 © 578foot | Dreamstime.com

p. 75 © Michael Flippo | Dreamstime.com

p. 82 © Andrey Kiselev | Dreamstime.com

p. 95 © Daniel Wiedemann | Dreamstime.com

p. 100 © Aleksandar Kamasi | Dreamstime.com

p. 105 © Vladimir Ioselevich | Dreamstime.com

p. 109 © Mythja | Dreamstime.com

p. 115 © Cheryl Quigley | Dreamstime.com

p. 119 © Yuri Bershadsky | Dreamstime.com

p. 124 © Bolotov | Dreamstime.com

p. 126 © Andrey Kiselev | Dreamstime.com

p. 136 © Maxpro | Dreamstime.com

p. 145 © Torsten Schon | Dreamstime.com

p. 150 © Magouillat | Dreamstime.com

p. 163 © Lali Kacharava | Dreamstime.com

p. 168 © Agg | Dreamstime.com

p. 177 © Blotty | Dreamstime.com

p. 184 © Carlo Cataeno | Dreamstime.com

p. 188 © Konstantin Kirillov | Dreamstime.com

p. 194 © Budda | Dreamstime.com

p. 198 © Scott Karcich | Dreamstime.com

p. 208 © Stefano Tiraboschi | Dreamstime.com

p. 212 © Péter Gudella | Dreamstime.com

p. 228 © Konstantins Visnevskis | Dreamstime.com

Back photograph © Morpheusm | Dreamstime.com

Dr Tarja Moles is an author and a writer. Originally from Finland, she now lives in Devon, UK, with her husband.

Lightning Source UK Ltd.
Milton Keynes UK
UKOW07f2326290715

256019UK00010B/289/P